MUSIC
AND THE
COSMIC
DANCE

MUSIC
AND THE
COSMIC
DANCE

Cynthia Serjak, RSM

WITH A FOREWORD
BY
MATTHEW FOX, OP

THE PASTORAL PRESS
WASHINGTON, DC

ISBN: 0-912405-31-7

© The Pastoral Press, 1987

The Pastoral Press
225 Sheridan Street, NW
Washington, D.C. 20011
(202) 723-1254

The Pastoral Press is the Publications Division of the National Association of Pastoral Musicians, a membership organization of musicians and clergy dedicated to fostering the art of musical liturgy.

Printed in the United States of America.

Contents

Part Four
Musicology for a New Creation

Foreword

I welcome this exciting invitation by Cynthia Serjak to explore and enter into the *Music and the Cosmic Dance*. In this book Cynthia is not just advising her sister and brother musicians and artists about directions they can and need to take. She is doing much more. She is herself taking on the responsibility of contributing to a living cosmology. Thus, she is acting as a prophet within the world of art and of liturgy itself. For if there is one thing that sadly characterizes the demise of worship in the West over the past few centuries, it has been the awful anthropocentricism that has relegated cosmology to a peripheral matter. What is the result? Often lack of mystery, lack of adventure, lack of challenge. Sentimentalism and superficiality have tended to dominate worship during the Newtonian era of culture and religion. Instead of unleashing the powers of people that a living cosmology excites, the predictable result of worship without cosmos is more often than not a combination of boredom and frustration—boredom because religion without cosmology is flat and trite; frustration because deep down the worshipper knows that worship is not about trivial matters—yet he or she often finds worship experience to be quite trivial indeed.

The contribution of Cynthia Serjak is to lay the groundwork for the directions to which artists are called in a time like ours when a cosmology is emerging again. She probes the new creation story that today's science is giving us, and she probes the mystical dimensions of music, art, and a recovery of a theology of the Cosmic Christ. I understand a living cosmology to be the coming together in merry dance and powerful vision of three elements in culture: Science, Art, and Mysticism. Serjak's call to co-creation is well taken, for a cosmology is not something one *fits into*—we have had enough of machine-like models from the recent Newtonian era. A living cosmology is something one participates in by creating and co-creating with self, nature, God. And with those who study nature—scientists; and those who challenge the depths of human nature—mystics; and those who articulate in images that excite and move others—artists. Mysticism becomes the internalizing of the cosmos within the human psyche; and art is the manifestation of the internalized cosmos. In such a context the people are no longer bored and worship can never be trivialized. In this book Serjak offers ample food to challenge artists within and without churches; also liturgists; and all who go to worship or wish to go but find themselves excluded by reason of worship's Newtonian air.

What constitutes this "Newtonian air" of worship of which I speak? Mechanism; reductionism; atomism; anthropocentrism. Newton pictured the universe as a machine. Since his time much liturgy has been operating on a machine-model. Ritual becomes rendered as rote memorizing (or reading) of texts, and a kind of dispenser-of-grace mentality pervades the sense of a waning sacramental power. Newton reduced knowledge of the whole to knowledge of parts, and there is a distinct parts-mentality to liturgy wherein each "part" is meant to be performed in a "correct" manner. But the full whole—the cosmic whole—is left out. Reductionism prevails when parts are mistaken for the whole. And triviality is the result. Of course one instance of atomism and parts-over-whole mentality is anthropocentrism itself—which mistakes that part of creation called human for the whole—which is vastly more amazing than just the two-legged ones. The idea that to worship one must be able to read has prevailed of late: reading Scriptures, reading prayers, reading hymns. But only humans read, and among them the very young do not read. Today in America some 37 percent of adults are functionally illiterate (compared to 2 percent in Cuba, for example). Thus, this reading mentality in worship kills the power and soul of mysticism, of shared silence, of the depths from which music arises. And all other signs of Divinity. For if, as Eckhart teaches, "God is a great underground river," then there must be space and openness and silence in our worship to allow Divinity in.

I welcome therefore the significant challenge that Cynthia Serjak throws out to theologian, artist, parish worker, and priest alike in this book. Do we care enough about liturgy to criticize it? To truly *renew* it and not merely reform it? It is telling that the first document of Vatican II was on liturgical reform. Perhaps it ought to have been the last document in order to profit from the other theological directions that documents such as *The Church in the Modern World* and that on *Non-Christian Religions* provided to church and society alike. Or, perhaps a true liturgical awakening will open the next Vatican Council to come. In any case, I feel deeply that Serjak in this book has named the issue very appropriately and with the passion of a prophet: the issue is the coming of a cosmology. One hopes that its arrival is not too late. One knows that it will take vital worship and authentic ritual to make this cosmology a living one. One is reminded of the hopeful promise from the prophet of old whom Cynthia Serjak cites:

> The vision still has its time,
> presses on to fulfillment,
> and will not disappoint. (Habakkuk 2:3)

This book does not disappoint. It does what its title claims. It invites us to a renewal of music by way of the cosmic dance. One is reminded of the vision of Hildegard of Bingen eight centuries ago who taught that "wisdom resides in all works of art." Hildegard believed that it was especially "through the power of hearing" that "God opens to human beings all the glorious sounds of the hidden mysteries and of the choirs of angels by whom God is praised over and over again . . . We would be empty were we not able to hear and comprehend." After all, the human soul "is a symphony" and "all of creation is a symphony of the Holy Spirit which is joy and jubilation."*

Matthew Fox, o.p.
Director, Institute of Culture
and Creation Spirituality
Holy Names College, Oakland, California

---

* Citations are Hildegard's words from Matthew Fox, *Illuminations of Hildegard of Bingen* (Santa Fe: Bear and Company, 1985) 115ff.

Preface

If one understands that human creatures are born of the
universe,
    and that our human tasks are an important and unique
        expression
of the energy and wisdom of that universe working in us,
then our first acknowledgement of gratitude, when the
work is
        done,
    must be addressed to the universe and its marvelously
        imaginative Creator.
If we have accomplished a significant task,
    it has surely been with the help of myriads of ancestors
    who have shaped who we are,
    how we think and feel,
    and what images and words we use.

And so I am grateful for all those creatures from whom I
have received what incomplete, though growing and deep-
ening, understandings of life and music which I have
attempted to share in this book. I am very grateful to my
brothers and sisters in the human community, especially:

—Matthew Fox, O.P., Brian Swimme, Starhawk, and all the
faculty and students at the Institute in Culture and Creation
Spirituality, all prophets and mystics in the ancient and wise
traditions of this universe;

—Virgil Funk, President of the National Association of
Pastoral Musicians; and Larry Johnson, Director of The
Pastoral Press, for support and encouragement in the
development and refinement of the manuscript;

—and the countless friends with whom I have tested ideas and images, and from whom I have received encouragement and challenge, especially Jim Bender, Rick Gibala, Mary Ann Pobicki, and Frank Sokol.

In the days before when
the song was flung out
through the space of forever—

Unleashed, as it were,
in a fire passion
of naked rhythm.

The music fire-battered
the rock of a planet
young and primarily exposed.

Air-softened,
Water-confronted,
The fire leapt
and was gone—

The song lies struck
in magic rock

Waiting.
Waiting.

Introduction

It may seem surprising to begin a book about music and spirituality with a chapter on cosmic connections. We are accustomed to descriptions of spirituality that begin by talking about God, and descriptions of music that speak of music as being made by and for people. This way of speaking implies that spirituality is something out there that we must go out to get (just like God is "out there"), and that music is something inside people that must be given to others who don't have it. Many people, like spiritual directors and music teachers, are beginning to realize that this attitude is no longer adequate to express what is really happening. Spirituality is not "out there" that we should find it apart from ourselves, nor is music only able to be heard and experienced by some people, or by people only. So we shall begin in another place.

Reflecting on the cosmos opens up our perspectives so that we can learn about and experience the universe and begin to look for ourselves there. It suggests to us that our concepts of God have been too small and that our tendency to begin history (including the history of music) with the arrival of the human species on the planet is too short-sighted. We must begin to see and hear back farther, back to our cosmic beginnings and farther out to our cosmic rhythms and melodies. This kind of work (or play) will wake us up to our task as humans as well as connect us with the vast amount of energy available to us as the children of the universe.

The contemporary story of the beginning of our cosmos, often referred to as the "New Story," describes the origins of our cosmos in an explosion of light, a fireball. This fireball filled the universe. All that we now know as universe was in that initial fire—including our sun, the stars, the planets, our

1

bodies, trees, animals, plants. That means that all of us, namely, all of the above, are related in a very origin-al way. We have a common ancestry, and we share the heritage of this universe with the stars as well as with the tiniest plants and the largest animals. If this scenario feels uncomfortable to us, if we tend to dismiss it, then we can stop to ask, "If we weren't all there, where were we? And when did we come in?" The New Story of the cosmos reintroduces us to our beginnings and to our connections to other cosmic events— the birth of planets, the dance of the stars, the movement of continents.

To say that we dance with the stars is to allow ourselves to be swept up in the excitement which this New Story generates. We are invited out of our anthropocentric stance toward the rest of creation and into the circle of life. We are challenged to know our origins in many mothers and fathers, the thousands of ancestors (not only people) who have given form and stuffing to what we now call human. We can reflect on our origins in the first fireball of creation, conceived in the eternal womb of the Creator. We find that the stars are our brothers and sisters, and in that recognition the dance begins.

To talk about our cosmic connections with the stars and planets is to activate our memory in a new way, in an imaginative way. We have some practice in imagining the future (What would it be like to have children, to move to the South Pacific? What will heaven be like?), but we also need to develop an imagination for the past, so that we can uncover and experience the mysteries of our origins. We should learn from all that has gone before us, so that we can participate in what is now happening around us and in us. What was the first burst of creation like? Where did the stars come from? How big or how small are we in the universe? Where are we going? And how do we get there safely?

Imagining should not be foreign to the human species, although it seems that we are dreadfully out of practice. We were created in the image of God (Genesis 1:27) who is the greatest Imaginer of all time. For God the Creator imagined the universe into existence, freely creating all that we know. And we are co-creators, co-imaginers. This divinely inherited creativity is sorely needed in a world community weighed down by many problems and few solutions. We need to imagine that we can feed those who are hungry, imagine that war is outdated, imagine that all creatures can be free to wonder at the marvel of existence. For in our imagining these wonders, the energy for their coming into reality is already unleashed.

The cosmos calls us out from our narrow person-only world view, into a universe-sized picture. We are asked to activate our imaginations as we remember the Creator, the originator, the grand designer, the first cosmic artist. In doing so, our spirituality will also have to open up and expand to embrace the creation rather than shut it out as a distraction. We see in creation brilliant images of our Creator, and draw from creation an energetic compassion for the human race to accomplish its good work of imagining a future of health for our planet. And so we realize that far from being "out there," spirituality is very "in here," among us, around us, inside us, in the universe, waiting to be discovered and nourished. This is surely "Good News"!

When we have imagined our cosmic connections, we long for a way to shape those images for sharing. Among the shapes from which to choose we discover music. While we are busy in the music-making, we may ask ourselves, "Where does the music come from?" Is it also sister and brother to us, born of the same Creator, propelled outward in the explosion of the cosmic fireball? What is our relationship to music? Do we create it, make it, or discover it? Do we find it or does it find us? Can we hear the hum of the turning planet as well as the music in the trees? Does the rhythm of exploding stars entice us as strongly as the pumping of the smallest creature-heart? Does the harmony of the universe sing out from our own bodies?

This book will not be a scientific study nor a historical one, although many references will be made to science and history. Readers are strongly encouraged to explore the sources which we will cite. Likewise, we will touch on theology, and reference will be made to experts in that field, particularly those theologians who are working with this newest cosmic story through their study and teaching of

3

creation-centered spirituality. But mostly this book will be about connections and conversions. Music will be our special vehicle in the exploration of cosmic connections, although there could be many others. Again, readers are encouraged to reflect on the ideas presented here in relation to other arts, work, and life activities. We will be working at connections among fields like science and theology that have been separate for too long. We will work at conversion from old ways of looking at the cosmos, life, spirituality, and music, to new ways of experiencing all of these. In this work new images will arise to teach us.

If we trust that we are all images of God, then we can welcome the co-creating excitement of our exploration. We can trust the new images that rise in us, and we can be ready to listen and be taught. The music of the universe is struck into the rock. It waits for an invitation, a calling-forth. It seeks instruments for playing and voices for singing; it needs hand and heart and body to be created. What are we waiting for?

PART I

We Dance with the Stars
Discovering Our Cosmic Connections

Introduction

As human beings of the twentieth century we have inherited a wealth of material from those who have gone before us. And so we do not have to start from scratch to discover our cosmic connections. However, we may have to work hard to remove our twentieth century blinders—the blinders of sophistication and rationality which may limit our sight as we review the stories of our primal ancestors. But the hard work of opening our eyes to the world can only be helpful to us as we realize that human presence on earth represents only a fraction of the planet's history. What can it mean for us to be such a young species? We have a lot to learn. Why not begin with the wisdom accumulated by all those who have gone before us? Perhaps it will be more a work of remembering and awakening, of evoking wisdom that is already within us.

And so we begin our exploration with stories, creation "myths." By retracing the ideas and images of our ancient ancestors, perhaps we can recapture some of their excitement and wonder for this planet and universe. Without dismissing or forgetting our own valuable scientific data, and in fact by keeping it close at hand, we may rediscover some important insights which will serve us well as we struggle to survive as a planetary community.

1

Science, Art, and Theology
Welcome the New Story
of the Universe

> The eastern mystics see the universe as an inseparable
> web, whose interconnections are dynamic and not static.
> The cosmic web is alive, it moves, grows and changes
> continually. Modern physics, too, has to come to con-
> ceive of the universe as such a web of relations and, like
> Eastern mysticism, has recognized that this web is
> intrinsically dynamic.[1]

We are familiar with many of the ancient stories of the
origins of the universe: Genesis (Hebrew Scripture), En-
numa Elish (Babylonia), the cosmic egg (India, China,
Polynesia, and many others). We call these stories "myths."
Unfortunately the word myth has become a victim of a
particular contemporary mindset that wants to know "reality," a reality that is scientifically verifiable and factual, able
to be proven, sensible and clear. In this mindset myth is often
considered to be synonymous with fiction as a "made-up"
story which is not "true." In religious spheres myth may also
connote a story for the unsophisticated or even the super-
stitious. If we can clear away our suspicions that myth is
trying to fool us, we can see that most of these creation
stories are a response to the universe, a world view, a way of
explaining how things are and how they came to be. "The
myth relates a sacred history . . . But to relate a sacred history
is equivalent to revealing a mystery."[2] The creation myth is a
story which tells a mysterious history—how things came to
be as we find them. Although the data about a particular life
situation may be written in definitive style, myth, by its

descriptive imaginative language, paints a picture in our minds and engages our experience within the event revealed in the myth. Myths of the cosmos help us to imagine the universe and our relationship to it.

Let us take two creation stories, one a primal myth and the second a version of the New Story.

A Maori Cosmogony

Io dwelt within breathing-space of immensity.
The Universe was in darkness, with water everywhere.
There was no glimmer of dawn, no clearness, no light.
And he began by saying these words,—
That he might cease remaining active:
   "Darkness, become a light-possessing darkness."
And at once light appeared.
(He) then repeated those self-same words in this manner,—
That he might cease remaining inactive:
   "Light, become a darkness-possessing light."
And again an intense darkness supervened.
Then a third time He spake saying:
   "Let there be one darkness above,
   Let there be one darkness below (alternate).
   Let there be a darkness unto Tupua,
   Let there be a darkness unto Tawhito;
   It is a darkness overcome and dispelled.
   Let there be one light above,
   Let there be one light below (alternate).
   Let there be a light unto Tupua,
   Let there be a light unto Tawhito.
   A dominion of light,
   A bright light."
And now a bright light prevailed...

These words (of Io) became impressed on the minds of our ancestors, and by them were they transmitted down through the generations. Our priests joyfully referred to them as being:
   "The ancient and original sayings.
   The ancient and original words.
   The ancient and original cosmological wisdom.

Which caused growth from void.
The limitless space-filling void,
As witness the tidal-waters,
the evolved heaven,
The birth-given evolved earth... "[3]

And from the New Story:

Imagine that furnace out of which everything came
forth. This was a fire that filled the universe—that *was*
the universe. There was no place in the universe free
from it. Every point of the cosmos was a point of this
explosion of light. And all the particles of the universe
churned in extremes of heat and pressure, all that we
see about us, all that now exists was there in the
beginning, in that great burning explosion of light....

Most amazing is this realization that everything that
exists in the universe came from a common origin. The
material of your body and the material of my body are
intrinsically related because they emerged from and
are caught up in a single energetic event. Our ancestry
stretches back through the life forms into the stars,
back to the beginnings of the primeval fireball. This
universe is a single multiform energetic unfolding of
matter, mind, intelligence, and life. [4]

Both of these stories capture our imagination. The sense
of primordial darkness, explicit in the earlier version, is
implicit in the later version (what was there before the
furnace?). In the first story Io speaks "that he might cease
remaining inactive." Activity is a clear and significant
characteristic of the New Story. The beginnings of the
universe released lots and lots, and millions and millions of
years worth, of activity. The bright light, the fireball—one
an intuitive experience, one based on scientific data.

We can see the light from the primeval fireball. Or at
least the light from its edge, for it burned for nearly a
million years. We can see the dawn of the universe
because light from its edges reached us only now, after
traveling twenty billion years to get here. [5]

9

The Maori tradition tells of "growth from the void." The newest story is that "everything that exists came from a common origin." We compare "the evolved heaven" with "a single multiform energetic unfolding." Both stories speak of original unity, of process rather than product: "The birth-given evolved earth" and, more scientifically, "matter, mind, intelligence and life."

And so we find ourselves in a wonderful moment: What primal people intuited about the universe is now being described by scientists as "reality." This realization offers us a new sense of history, a dynamic rather than a linear sense. Spiraling around our linear timetable is the unfolding, the evolving, the energy, and the creativity of an outgoing and dynamic universe. It is as if by reaching back to reawaken the beauty and excitement of those primal myths and laying them alongside our contemporary science, all of cosmic history is swirling before us, still engaged in that bursting forth from the spoken word, the unleashed energy of the act of Creation. The universe has been waiting for time to unfold itself and for the human species to wake up to allowing its vast beauty, its vast glory as well as its intricate detail, to be shown and celebrated. We have come to the point of understanding that simply telling the scientific data about what's going on around us is not enough, just as listing dates and events in a person's life does not make a biography. What waits to be told are the stories that connect and enliven the data, for that is where the wonder lies. We know that there are vast continents on our planet. We can name and count them. But the stories of how those continents broke apart and collided and formed give us new eyes to see "our country." Over and over again the New Story affirms what ancient myths teach: we are very connected, in origin, in matter, in energy, in ancestry. When we hear the primal stories about those connections, we realize that we have come to an incredible moment: it is as if all of wisdom and myth, all the ancient stories and philosophies and theologies are catching up with us, dancing around us, waiting for us to see and celebrate the connections that science can now confirm.

Rather than feeling alienated from the past or arrogant

10

about the immense intellectual prowess of the human animal, we are called by the New Story of the cosmos to an appropriate humility—an appreciation of our origins in the universe, and more particularly, in this earth. It is no wonder that the more we realize about our origins the more we recollect earlier names: Mother Earth and cosmic egg. It is the data which can satisfy the curiosity of our minds, but the myth that will connect and convert us.

Perhaps we may feel a tug of regret since this realization makes us rethink our assumptions about progress. We have called the early humans "primitive." But we have none of their excitement for dancing with stars and circling with the planets. We have lost the connection with the energy of the burst of creation. We have forgotten to wonder and celebrate. Might they not call us poor, underdeveloped . . . primitive?

An example of this lack of connectedness with our cosmic story is the separation that exists between science and religion, occurring particularly in the last four centuries. Rather than being companions in our planetary endeavor, science and religion have gone their own separate ways, theology scandalized at where science is leading us, and science embarrassed at theology's unwillingness to face its technological revelations. A new partnership between science and theology must be initiated. Science needs theology to reflect on its data, to work with its conscience, to name its wonder and to offer it stories. We witness a tremendous creative activity on the part of science. But products of that creativity can be divine or demonic, health or harm for the planetary community. Who will call science to task for the use of its creative talent to promote destruction? Who is more creative than the military empire, whose inventions threaten not only the life that exists now but all life to come? Many of the issues involved are new—we have not before had the power to blow up the entire planet and destroy all future possibilities of life. In a nuclear holocaust we not only kill life, we kill the chance for birth.[6] Our cosmologists and physicists have to dialogue with our mystics and theologians so that this serious question, as well as many others which plague us, may be addressed.

11

And what about the ordinary "religious" person, the person who lives in the world of technology that science has created and worships in an institution that does not address that world? So many people who have a strong religious commitment feel powerless to do anything about the problems that surround us. Young people in particular are not feeling hopeful about their futures. The churches offer them little or nothing to encourage them to be hopeful enough to be creative. It is not a blind faith that we need, nor a conviction that the elect will be swept up and saved at the last moment. We need a faith, a theology, a spirituality that helps us to meet and dialogue with the problems that greet us in our daily world: the pollution of our air and water, the shredding of our forests, the loss of valuable topsoil, the elimination of species after species, the waste and contamination and abuse of our planet's resources and creatures.

Our spirituality should put us in touch with the problems which science and the media often lull us into thinking are not there, or are not solvable. We have begun to think that no matter what the problem, sooner or later, with enough money and research, there will be an answer. Theology should deal with questions about the quality of life in this scientific age, and remind us that spirituality is "in here," and that as religious people we should wake up to what is going on around us. We need to challenge the assumption that science has an answer for everything, including its own creations (for example, nuclear waste). Theologians ought to reflect with scientists about our connectedness, the importance of cherishing life, the task and privilege of the human species as image of God, as co-creator, as steward of creation. But religion seems to leave us in a vacuum when it comes to scientific (or political) issues. The common person feels powerless against the military machine and the incomprehensibility of technology. Where are the prophets among us who will keep raising the life-saving questions? Our spirituality has been too small if it has encouraged us to close in on ourselves, looking only for personal salvation; our religion has failed us if we cannot see the reality of the world around us.

Who will help us imagine what the origins of the cosmos were like, as well as reflect on and critique the newest discoveries of our scientific era? Science is greatly in need of artists, those who paint the pictures, make the sounds, weave the colors of the cosmological story. We are not yet able to take photographs of the whole cosmos, although our ability to see and portray the universe keeps expanding. But artists can help us with that kind of immensity. We cannot hear the movement of planets, but music can help us experience their harmony and their play. We have no film of the emergence of life, but dance can connect us with those primal movements. We do not know the color or space of the stars, but all kinds of paint can invite us into a universe of colors.

The imagination of artists can help us experience the divine as well as the demonic possibilities of our technological endeavor. In August 1985, in various places in the United States, groups of artists staged a Shadow Project in which the outlined figures of those obliterated in the Hiroshima bombing in World War II were drawn on city sidewalks. People were startled to be walking over the "shadow remnants" of those sisters and brothers caught in the devastation. This kind of "art" can give us space to reflect on the implications of technology for the quality of our lives. It can confront us with what we may not wish to see with our eyes or what we may be too afraid to imagine.

If science is in need of theology and art to reflect it and reflect on it, so theology is in need of science and the arts, although for somewhat different reasons. Theology needs the concrete questions of science to keep it open and growing. Theologians must address the questions that face our planet if they are to be credible in this generation. Can technology motivate itself to stop polluting the planet? Or will it continue to kill off species of life every day, species which never will again reappear? Can theology call science to task for its irresponsibility to creation and its rampant thirst for knowledge and "progress," often attained at the sacrifice of someone's life? We cannot erase centuries of technology nor ignore the vast good it can accomplish. But the time for separation and specialization is past. When we speak about the human community, the planet, all of creation, we must include the wonders of technology, but also the compassion and life-sustaining vision of theology. When people look to churches for guidance in issues of justice their questions must not continue to go unanswered.[7]

For many centuries the churches have been patrons as well as benefactors of the arts. Whether or not theology has seen art as its partner, however, is debatable. Although some of the most universally celebrated works of art are "religious" in theme, theology has not always welcomed art as an expression of its own truth. More significantly, many artists find religious institutions confining and naive. Their lives, often on the fringes of church and society, are suspect; they seem to maintain a different schedule of time and remain unimpressed with doctrinal preaching. Connections need to be made between the artistic process and the life project, the themes of art and the themes of theology. Theology needs art to flesh out its ideas, to give color and shape and sound to its amazing mysteries, to struggle with its questions. Most especially theology needs art to enliven its rituals, to open up the richness of its symbols. Even the steps made in this direction during the current Christian liturgical renewal seem very hesitant, theology always maintaining its distance and its firm and singular hold on truth and orthodoxy, or being more concerned with moral issues than ritual ones. As long as religion insists on black and white answers (sin or not-sin, God or not-God), art will be suspect, for art always wants to present the flip-side, the shadow, the other sound, the forgotten movement. When others want to settle on answers, art is asking new questions.

A sign of maturity in the human species is the ability to be open and resilient, to be willing to listen to many viewpoints, to celebrate many cultures and ideas, not to tighten up and shut down in the face of adversity. When you are mature (whole) you realize that what is "you" is not threatened by what is "not-you"; rather the not-you can be recognized, respected, tested, and learned from. Too often religion's task has been one of defense, defining doctrine and reciting creed, rather than listening and dialoguing. All membership had to do was believe the truth presented and it could be sure of being right and saved. In this history there was no acceptance of doubt, no healthy dialogue, no ragged edges. The New Story calls us all to grow up and welcome other viewpoints, including all the ragged edges of human experience, not as competitors, not as suspect or threatening, but as partners and friends in the full circle of creation. This kind of partnership would promote an atmosphere of mutual critique as well as mutual respect and responsibility for working on the problems of the world community.

If the arts are to be helpful to science in portraying the cosmic story and to theology for reflecting its mysteries, then artists must be welcomed back into the life of the community. Why has art not been at the center of life? Part of the answer has to do with the development of an elitist image of artists. Both sides—that is, artists and non-artists alike—have contributed to this unfortunate state. For example, in the sixteenth and seventeenth centuries the work world became a separate space from the living space. The creative acts normally engendered and passed on in the family were removed from that arena. People began to buy rather than make, so they might be free to do another "job" which for some lucky few may have been as rewarding as the more creative and personally stamped tasks at home. Specialization and assembly line production remove the worker from the pleasure of admiring the works of hands, or seeing a process through to completion. People were robbed of the opportunity to learn the artistic process and learn what it has to teach about life processes.[8] Only the people who were "talented" could make a living by being creative and actually doing art. Other people began to see their work as uncreative, and although some leisure time activities make this connection, the word "artist" is generally applied to only a separate and elite group. Unfortunately this is still very true. The word "artist" became a job description rather than a naming of one side of everyone's life. Comments like "I'm not creative," or "I can't even draw a straight line," are indicative of the high level of misunderstanding about what art is, how it happens, and what makes art valuable to us.

15

Art has to do with experiencing and expressing connections. Sometimes the connections are made through surprises and juxtapositions (as in a sudden key change in music, or the arrangement of color in the painting). The listener/observer/doer is invited into a creative moment because the art piece needs the listener/observer/doer to help make the connection. In responding to this invitation the participant becomes unselfconscious, is "lost" to time and perhaps surroundings, while living inside the time and space of the art work. In this way the participant can experience a kind of mystical time, a connecting, inspiring, overwhelming time-out-of-time. This sort of threshold experience which art can evoke is very valuable for the task at hand. It is akin to the vision quests of Native Americans, to the initiation rituals of many primal people, when the young person is sent apart from the group to have an in-depth life experience. The mystical moment of art or of ritual widens our eyes to take in more reality and to see things in perspective. Part of that widening includes connecting to the reality that life presents, learning from it, and appreciating it.

These moments of vision, of clarity, and waking up need not be evoked only through joy. They often surprise us in times of intense grief or pain or confusion. When we "bottom out" we can learn what it is that is most valuable in our lives, what we can let go of, what we need to cultivate. We can learn all of this, but the process is not automatic. Art should help us into experiences of mysticism, vision, and conversion. Art invites us to imagine new things, expands our wealth of ideas for dealing with what life presents to us, offers connections to all facets of creation.[9]

Art is very related to mysticism, and mysticism is very related to prophecy. Spirituality that results in "the soul's union with God" but disregards the rest of humanity (not to mention the rest of creation) is not particularly helpful to the project of making connections. Those who go on vision quests, who have threshold moments, return to the community to speak about what they have seen and to act upon the wisdom of the vision.[10] We need art and mysticism that result in serious critique of what's happening and creative

16

ideas for survival. Just as the religious person cannot ignore the critical problems of this time, so the serious artist cannot rest on his or her mystical reputation, but must get into dialogue with those in other fields who are working at planetary survival. Science needs a mirror in which to see itself—its wonders as well as its horrors, its healing as well as its destructive power. If art is elitist and mystically unrelated, science could call it to work, to keep its mysticism prophetic, to help us to see, hear, feel, taste, and touch the wonder that science reveals for us.

Art can go in another direction—being very prophetic but losing its mystical footing. This can easily happen in a society that makes darlings of certain artists because of a unique style, personality, or message.[11] The prophesying may continue, but the message loses depth and conviction, and works may be multiplied on the basis of past successes. Or in other cases artists become short-lived heroes, burned out before they are fully developed. (This can also happen to prophets in other fields, for example, social justice activists whose work has no mystical grounding.)

If art rants and raves in tongues but is not grounded in life experience and does not address that experience, then who will call it to task? It could be theology. A vibrant and prophetic theology will see the value of partnership with art in speaking out of a cultivated and healthy mysticism. Together theologians and artists could reflect on life issues, and as the former might use the word to prophesy, so the latter can use paint and clay and sound and gesture.

The model for this new partnership of theology, science, and the arts must be circular rather than ladder-like. There can be no priority of ownership, of material, of truth. All fields (including others like education, law, and medicine) must come to see the importance of working with and learning from each other. The wisdom and experience of various disciplines will not lose ground by being passed around, but in fact will most likely be enriched. On a ladder-like model of working, this kind of sharing is difficult (you have to let go of the ladder with one hand at least) and much less likely. Rather, a circular model illustrates how wisdom can be passed around as well as tossed back and forth across the circle. The image that Fritjof Capra (in the opening quote of this chapter) offers us, that of a web, is also helpful. Capra's work reflects the contemporary discovery that what people have intuited about the connections of this universe is what science is now discovering as fundamental. In addition to the contributions from the East which Capra cites, there are also Western mystics who name the experience of that same web of life, mystics such as Meister Eckhart.

Apprehend God in all things,
for God is in all things.

Every single creature is full of God
and is a book about God.

Every creature is a word of God.

If I spent enough time with the tiniest creature—
even a caterpillar—
I would never have to prepare a sermon.
So full of God is every creature.[12]

Or Hildegard of Bingen.

The air, blowing everywhere serves all creatures.
Ever is the firmament its support.
Ever it is held, carried, by the power of God.[13]

Fortunately these Christian mystics, so long ignored or forgotten in the Western spiritual tradition, are being rediscovered in our own time and their works are being made available to us.[14]

We have touched upon many images for the reconnection of science, theology, and art (a dance, a circle, a web). Perhaps it would be helpful at this point to consider how this reconnecting might affect an aspect of one's approach to life. For this consideration we will examine the health of the human body. Recent trends in wholistic health care make us aware of the importance of giving attention to the various aspects of the human body within the context of the whole system. Although scientifically determined data may be helpful in discovering the nature of health problems, physical treatment of the problem should occur within the context of the whole patient. In fact, attention to and treatment of the physical problem out of that context may prove detrimental. Or treatment of only one aspect of the physical body may influence other aspects. One medication can debilitate another, or the combination of two medications can cause a new problem or reaction. This kind of treatment is based on a "parts" mentality and attitude which has permeated not only medicine but our whole world view, our educational systems, and our religious experience. We go one place to treat ailments of the soul and another to treat ailments of the body. Without denying the legitimacy of the medical system, we must admit that too often the symptom (pain, for example) is addressed without considering what is the problem. Or the problem is treated, rather than the patient. In fact, this kind of health care starts with the problem rather than with the patient.

This parts mentality is often referred to as "Newtonian" since it takes its cue from Newton's parts concept of the universe. Though this mentality was not original, sometime between 1500 and 1700 "the organic concept of the cosmos gave way to a mechanistic one."[15] As science grew into a recognizable and separate field, it lost its connections with the more mystical naming of the web of the universe. Nevertheless, its images began to be applied to other fields: for example, William Harvey referred to the human heart as a pump. The world view became our body view, and the body became a machine. This allowed for the treatment of a body part without reference to the whole, and presumed the need for "fixing" from an external agent rather than encouraging the body's own inner healing process to function.

Fortunately as we rediscover that we are more like the cosmic web—breathing, alive, flexible—than a cosmic machine, we can also recover a more organic image for our human bodies.[16] With reflection (in the company of mystics and artists) we can redeem the human body from a parts-focused health care system, and refuse to submit to a machine-fixing approach. Theology teaches us reverence for the human body. In the wide variety of creation stories (especially in Genesis) we hear of the emergence of the human as an awesome event. Our bodies were formed from the earth, and as we reverence our bodies we are reminded to reverence the earth that gave them shape. We learn that part of the task of good stewards of creation is to see that our bodies are fed properly (including not too much), exercised sufficiently and generally kept in good order. This requires not only the data (weight, protein intake, blood pressure, and so on) but also an inner attuning to the body's health. A wholistic approach includes a trust that the body will know what it needs, and that the body is the single most powerful source of its own healing. [17]

A spirituality that distrusts or puts down the body, that focuses primarily on the body's "fall," that overemphasizes "soul" (a distinction that primal people would not have understood) will not object to health care that continues to treat the body as something to be acted upon rather than worked with. On the other hand, a spirituality that celebrates the human body (as spiritualities for incarnational theologies should) will call health care systems to task for this kind of "parts" mentality. Likewise it will call planetary systems to task for their ill-treatment of the earth. The human body deserves our "undivided" attention. This does not mean that we should all be hypochondriacs. But it does mean that we are attentive to the body's signs of what kind of care is appropriate to its health. It also encourages us to look to the earth's own history and processes for clues about being good citizens of the planet.

The important work of reclaiming the body's good health can be aided by the arts, since a parts approach to art is dreadfully inappropriate. The work of the painting includes the sensitive placement of color and shape, the wise use of line and texture. All of those pieces are woven together in such a way to create a whole. It is this whole—the finished piece—which first addresses the viewer. The discriminating observer may approach more closely to notice technique; but then the viewer steps back again to see how the details work together to make the piece whole. The human form presents itself as a whole, although upon observation the details quickly show themselves. To remove or change one of those details immediately affects the whole. The painting and the person are changed when something about them or in them is changed. Both the painting and the person have a life of their own, an intrinsic and dynamic unity, a wholeness.

What is needed now is for the arts, the sciences, the technologies, and the theologies to lay aside separatism and elitism and join in the cosmic circle to share the good news of their various workings. The human body provides an up-close example of what this could mean; it is an analogical microcosm for this joining together. What can give us an analogy for a body of macrocosmic significance? What will help us imagine a rediscovery of our connectedness in a global way? What will help us stop preaching our own story so loudly and begin listening to the fine rhythms of other cultures and creatures? What will challenge us to work together with others rather than seek power over them? What image will excite us and allure us into cosmic dancing?

Ladies and Gentlemen, all Friends in the Circle of
   Creation,
We offer you: The Art of Music

2

Music As the Model
for a Global Civilization

The fundamental symbol for the classical scientific
world view was the billiard table with the billiard balls
glancing off one another. The fundamental symbol for
the world view that has emerged from the twentieth
century theoretical physics is that of the musical symphony. Though a careful understanding of quantum
physics demands an understanding of its mathematics,
the symbol that best grasps the new world view implicit
in mathematics is the symphony, the world itself as
symphony.[1]

One could ask the question, "What is music?" In our
classical scientific mindset (Newtonian) we have described
music as "made up of" three elements: rhythm, melody, and
harmony. And yet we would admit that when one hears
music, something more is happening than the simple combination of elements. The formula "1 + 1 + 1 = 3" is not an
adequate description of what happens in music-making. Nor
are the three elements heard separately from one another.
Rhythm, melody, and harmony work together, flow together, all showing their power and character as subjects in
the music-making.

The word music comes from the Greek *mousike* where it is
classified in the feminine gender because of the sister
goddesses in Greek mythology who preside over poetry and
song. Greek mythology describes the divine origins of
music, and gives to its gods (Apollo, Pan, Orpheus) musical
skills and creativity. In many ancient cultures music is used

extensively in ritual; songs of evoking gods and goddesses, songs of healing, songs of purification, all indicate the importance of the art and the power of music in primal world views.

Many examples can be found to help answer the question, "What is music?" In some cases the creator is described as a grand musician. Athanasius the great Christian bishop of Alexandria offers us this picture:

> For just as though one were to hear from a distance a lyre, composed of many diverse strings, and marvel at the concord of its symphony, in that its sound is composed neither of low notes exclusively, nor high nor intermediate only, but all combine their sounds in equal balance—and would not fail to perceive from this that the lyre was not playing itself, nor even being struck by more persons than one, but that there was one musician, even if he did not see him, who by his skill combined the sound of each string into the tuneful symphony; so the order of the whole universe being perfectly harmonious, and there being no strife of the higher against the lower or the lower against the higher, and all things making up one order, it is consistent to think that the Ruler and King of all Creation is one and not many, who by his own light illumines and gives movement to all.[2]

This theme of the creator of the universe as musician is taken up by Kabir, the fifteenth century Indian poet.

> Listen friend, this body is his dulcimer.
> He draws the strings tight, and out of it comes the
>   music of the inner universe.
> If the strings break the bridge falls,
> then this dulcimer of dust goes back to dust.[3]

Another mystic, this one Christian and female, portrays God as the music-maker and people as the instruments.

> As the Godhead
>   strikes the note
>   humanity sings.

24

The Holy Spirit is the harpist
and all the strings must sound
which are strung in love.[4]

Finally, in our own time, J.R. Tolkein offers us a very rich text which imagines God as composer, conductor, and orchestrator.

> Eru, the One called Ilúvatar spoke:
> ... propounding to them themes of music; and they sang before him and he was glad. But for a long while they sang only each alone, or but few together, while the rest harkened; for each comprehended only that part of the mind of Ilúvatar from which he came, and in the understanding of their brethren they grew but slowly. Yet even as they listened they came to deeper understanding, and increased in unison and harmony.
>
> ... and they saw a new World made visible before them, and it was globed amid the Void, and it was sustained therein, but was not of it. And as they looked and wondered this World began to unfold its history, and it seemed to them that it lived and grew...
>
> Ilúvatar said again: "Behold your music! This is your minstrelsy ... "[5]

Taking a cue from these ancestors and mystics, let us forgo the academic descriptions of the elements of music (these descriptions are plentiful in other sources) and ready ourselves for an experience of the power and mystery of music as a cosmic and original event. A description of the power of music's elements leaves much unsaid—but in mystery that is entirely appropriate.

The Power of the Elements of Music

Rhythm

We experience rhythm in many natural ways: our own heartbeat, the movement and change of seasons, the wash of waves on the shore, falling rain, day and night, sowing and reaping. Beyond these "natural" rhythms are others which human people have established: time-keeping, meal-sharing, work, rituals for morning (bathing, dressing, and the like).

Where did we get our tendency to work and play and live in rhythm?[6] Rather than inventing it, we humans may well have discovered it as already present within us and around us in creation. From our own primal heartbeat to the daily replenishment of our body cells to the rhythms of our growing and aging, we learn the power of repetition, variation, discipline and pattern. In the macrocosm creation teaches us its own rhythms, particularly in the dying and rising which are the preeminent rhythms of our planet. Within that basic rhythm there are hundreds of variations: some plants come up again in the spring after winter's ice and others don't. Trees take on various dying signs in autumn, but only after many winters do they finally die. The world freezes some of its embryos for safe-keeping through the winter, and others it recycles into mineral food. This dying and rising rhythm is intense and mysterious, and as the rite of spring unfolds we witness the always surprising rhythms of new life breaking through our frozen and unhopeful-looking wintertime.

Rhythm has become an important element in the New Story. For contemporary science tells us that names like "solid object" or "inanimate matter" are no longer adequate names for the reality of material. Rather, physicists tell us that all matter is a dance, some movements more subtle than others, but, nonetheless, dance. The atom is movement, rhythm, excitement. We must not allow the limitations of our human eyes to blur the reality. We can now engage our imaginations to think about and wonder at the primal dance in all matter.

> Modern physics has shown that the rhythm of creation and destruction is not only manifest in the turn of the seasons and in the birth and death of all living creatures, but is also the very essence of organic matter. According to the quantum field theory, all interactions between the constituents of matter take place through the emission

and absorption of virtual particles. More than that, the dance of creation and destruction is the basis of the very existence of matter, since all material particles "self-interact" by emitting and reabsorbing virtual particles. Modern physics has thus revealed that every subatomic particle not only performs an energy dance, but also is an energy dance, a pulsating process of creation and destruction.[7]

Perhaps we are not then "making" rhythm so much as revealing it, connecting with it, getting into it. We respond to the invitation of the universe to dance with it. We give that rhythm a particular shape when we make it into music. Rhythm gives a piece of music a unique and identifiable character. Rhythm enables us to make music together. Singers and players "catch" the rhythm from the conductor or from one another. When we choose to make music, we align ourselves with the rhythm of the composition, whether it is a one-hundred-year-old symphony or a spontaneous jazz improvisation. Rhythm is so essential to music-making that without it the communal project of playing or singing together could not work.

Rhythm enables people to sing together. The extended rhythms in phrases cause them to breathe together. This is not an insignificant work, for there is nothing more personal, more intimate to each of us than our life breath, that spirit inherited from generations and generations of rhythmic creatures, conceived and engendered in the rhythms of loving. No one else can contribute our own life breath for us. By choosing to enter the song, we put ourselves into the rhythm of the choir, or the assembly, or the folks around the fire, or the ritual circle.[8]

In a musical symphony some players use their life breath (wind instrument players) and some their muscle rhythm (strings and percussion, although often even these players are found to be breathing with the musical phrases). There can be several rhythmic patterns being played at once, but the symphony addresses the listener as an integrated work, as a whole. It lives and breathes like one wonderful organism. It needs the smooth functioning and appropriate beauty of its various parts (as in the human body) but the parts work and flow together to create what we recognize as "symphony."

If the musical symphony is to be a model for our global civilization, then we must ask the question: How can rhythm teach us to live as global citizens? Rhythm organizes us by way of invitation. When we hear the rhythm we are tempted to become involved in the music. Our hands clap, our toes tap, we sway, we dance. The rhythm catches us as we catch it. In the global vision we will be caught by the rhythm of a living organism called Earth. That rhythm is created, as in the musical symphony, by many, many rhythms, as hundreds of thousands of creatures respond to the Creator's invitation to cosmic dancing. Just as there can be a multitude of rhythms built into the symphonic movement, so there can be myriads of rhythms in this global creation, working together, dancing together, being caught up by the excitement of planetary living.

If we wish to enter the dance, we take up the rhythm of the music. That means laying aside our own particular rhythm for the excitement of a new one; it means allowing ourselves to be caught by the rhythm which offers itself in the music. If the prospect of global living is alluring enough, its rhythm may also catch us, helping to lay aside our own particular rhythm of living to enter the more enticing rhythm of global living. Or we could also bring our rhythm with us, contribute its vitality to the whole project, allow it to be in dialogue with other rhythms, so that it grows and changes. This often happens in a group activity, where the rhythm grows out of the people who are working together. There may be a conscious rhythmic plan, or the pace and flow of the work may emerge as the work begins. By choosing to be a part of that group rhythm we move a task toward completion, or share in the enjoyment of the dance or song, or are healed and refreshed in ritual. We always have the choice not to participate and to maintain a separate rhythm, just as we now have the choice to work at a global rhythm of living and dancing or to insist that such rhythm is impossible and undesirable. We also should note that being part of a group rhythm does not mean that when one leaves the group one has lost the rhythm that was contributed.

Musicians who have experienced the vitality of group rhythm do not go away empty, but are enlarged and strengthened in their own individual music-making activities. They learn from the group project, perhaps hear things in a new way, even are inspired to pursue ideas that may have been born in the group activity. In global or cosmic dancing the participants are also strengthened and refreshed for the return to their own rhythmic work.

Cosmic dancing is attested to both by scientists and by mystics.

> All creation,
> is awakened,
> called,
> by the resounding melody,
> God's invocation of the WORD. [9]

> I cannot dance, O Lord,
>   unless you lead me.
>   If you will
>   that I leap joyfully
>   then you must be the first to dance
>   and sing! [10]

> At last the notes of his flute come in,
> and I cannot stop from dancing around on the
> floor . . . [11]

This Creator-initiated cosmic dancing has revealed itself through the mystical experience and now through the scientific one. We find that contemporary scientists use somewhat "unscientific" language to describe their cosmic experience: "The creativity of the world is the throbbing emotion of the past hurling itself into a new transcendant fact." [12] The rhythm of the cosmos unfolding and spinning amazes the observer as much as the intimate dancing of the mystic with the loving Creator.

Melody

If rhythm demands a gift of ourselves in choosing to be a part of its vitality, melody is even more presumptuous.

Melody also has to do with the breath of life, but now the engagement is more costly: on my very life breath I spin out a tune. I release the breath in a disciplined fashion and on it weave an intelligible arrangement of sounds so that song is born. Without breath we cannot live. In melody we contribute our life breath to the song of the cosmos. As with rhythm, no one can do that for us. The choice and the gift are ours.

In melody we note contour, lines that move up or down, colors that are bright and sparkling or dark and dreamy, positive or negative. A melodic progression expands the field of sound and, in partnership with rhythm, results in something we recognize as "music." We may momentarily, deliberately, be aware of the rhythm, or at another moment, the melody; but for the most part we hear the whole—the music.

Combining rhythm and melody together means that as we begin to breathe together we also vibrate together as we share pitch. Far from rigid conformity this is wondrous unity, chosen participation in creating song that is always new, as the breath is new, as the choice is new. We risk being caught by the rhythm and melody. We risk being part of something much bigger than we are, something not to be controlled as much as to be with and in. As we are "in" love, so we are "in" music, "in" rhythm, "in" melody. In "Dry Salvages" from *The Four Quartets* T.S. Eliot wrote: " . . . you are the music while the music lasts."[13] We can say: you are the rhythm, you are the melody . . . you are the music. It is this rhythm and melody partnership that stays with us after the sound of the music-making has died away. The melody continues to sing inside us, and with the melody we remember the context of the song: the concert, the ritual, the party. The rhythm pulses on and sometimes distracts us. It is the rhythm-melody combination that helps us to recognize and remember the symphony. It is the tune used at worship that recurs to us in our times of personal meditation.

In a musical symphony there may be many melodies playing at once, weaving and interweaving, consonant or dissonant with one another, resembling more the play of ocean waves than the architecture of a building. The weaving is organic, alive, and flowing, rather than molded and set. Again, our attention may be drawn to a particular melody for a moment, but even in that moment we are aware that this melody is supported and surrounded by many others. We are drawn into hearing a second melody, then a third; and yet none of these melodies *is* the symphony. "Indeed, to speak of the leitmotif of the second movement of Beethoven's ninth as if this leitmotif could *be discussed in its entirety, in its fullness,* and *in all its meaning* without considering the whole from which it has been abstracted is an absurdity."[14]

Harmony

Already in the interweaving of melodies we find ourselves in the third element of music—harmony. Perhaps even more than rhythm and melody, harmony presents life to us and so can assist us in our global living. First, we need to be clear that harmony in music does not mean that all is peaceful and idyllic and that everyone is doing the same thing together. There are musical moments of unison, for example, when the choir sings a single melody line. But even in this unison we hear the blend of different timbres of voices and the different colors of male and female voices. Unison singing can be very effective and offer us a strong statement about standing together in song. However, people also enjoy singing in harmony. We could sing a hymn, where everyone is singing in the same or nearly the same rhythm, but in a different melodic line (soprano, alto, tenor, or bass). There is also great strength here. Times in our lives can be like this—everyone doing the same thing at the same time, but still offering their own flavor.

Polyphony, however, offers another model: in polyphony the voices sing something different in a different rhythm or at a different time. Perhaps this kind of music speaks most eloquently about the human experience of this age: people do different things at different times, in different ways. What is significant here is that polyphonic music is harmonious. The song could be cacophonous, but because there is mutual respect and discipline in the musical lines, the song becomes harmonious. Likewise our lives can feel disjointed and noisy, or they can flow, recognizing the beauty of different voices, rhythms, colors, personalities, and talents. Polyphony offers us an image for living together in harmony while being involved in lots of different works and projects.

On a personal level, people who are ill experience a breakup of the recognized patterns in their lives, a loss of trust in the give and take, an inability to see how their lives fit into the communal rhythm of family and friends, a feeling of out-of-stepness. Such people may benefit from the lessons of music because it reflects the give and take of life; it respects different melodies and their importance to the whole. This is why music can be therapeutic—not because it soothes and comforts, but because it is intricate, unpredictable, and challenging, and so is life. Music testifies that different sounds (and silence) can work together, that many melodies and harmonies can be woven into a great symphony. Far from losing their uniqueness, they are enhanced and celebrated for their contribution to the music. We need all of the rhythms, melodies, and harmonies for the playing of the symphony.

The implications of the model of musical harmony for the global civilization are abundant and clear: for people to live in harmony does not mean that things will be quiet and serene all the time, nor will the music of their life and work always sound consonant. Many songs that speak of peace imply that what we need is a return to Eden where darkness and dissonance will be banished. An experience of harmony in music does not indicate this. That kind of idyllic (and boring) vision for the planet is debilitating since a return to Eden and innocence is simply not possible. Once we realize this, we may feel betrayed by the false hope which such ideals offer and then lose our good energy for working for peace. Music can help us see our way toward a harmony that allows for dissonance and consonance, the interplay of individual rhythms and melodies, the celebration of all the parts of the global music.

On a broader scale, the incredible harmony of the universe, the way the stars live in relation to one another, the elemental forces (gravity, electro-magnetic, strong and weak nuclear reactions) which name how the universe is (not what it does)—can be an invitation not to settle for solutions to the planetary problems that dilute the harmony of our living. The best of science says: This is how the universe is, this is how we are meant to be, since we have been born of that universe. The best of music says: This is how music is, this lesson can be helpful to us, since music is one of the universe's ways of revealing who it is. We find that scientists and musicians can stand together in inviting us to a deeper consciousness about living together. In this they may well find themselves at odds with politicians who are still working at a nationalistic mindset, or even people in other professions who are reluctant to let go of old separatist or elitist notions.

The harmony of the universe invites us into its community. This means that the human community does not have to invent harmony. It is already present, not only in sound, but in the flow of energy, the give and take, the life and death of the universe. Within the harmony of the planet there is also dissonance—earthquakes, volcanoes, and droughts. As with music, we should not be lulled into thinking that there is no conflict in the universe. And, as with music, we planet people must learn that our melodies can be interwoven in global living, that our rhythm will be celebrated in the rhythmic gathering of this new civilization, that such harmony is far from boring or a blurring of differences, but is revealing of the wondrous and complex harmony that is cosmic life. Our new cosmology and a recovery of the power of the elements of music will call us—not back to Eden—but ahead to a global harmony which we have glimpsed, perhaps envisioned, but not yet heard or played.

If the music is a gift of the universe, if it comes to us through all kinds of creatures and reflects for us how the universe is, then we may ask: What is the role of the composer in music? Do we create music or discover it? Does it originate with us, or do we find it and reveal it? Where does the music come from? [15]

The older the source that we ask for answers to this question, the more we hear that music is something already around us, something "in the air" that people whom we call composers seem to be able to hear. Their life experience is heard and expressed in a variety of musical ideas, colors, tunes, and timbres. Some composers describe their hearing of the music as very mystical. We take as one example the contemporary French composer, Olivier Messiaen.

> Nature is primarily a very great power in which one can lose oneself, in a kind of nirvana, but above all it's a marvelous teacher, and this last aspect of it has been very useful to my work...

> I've listened with intense emotion to the waves of the sea, to the mountain torrents and waterfalls, and to all the sound made by water and wind. And I would add that I make no distinction between noise and sound; for me, all this represents music.[16]

Messiaen recognizes the mystical connection between himself and the universe around him, and in fact, when asked why he composes, answered: "...it seems to me that a composer writes because he must, because that is his vocation and he does it naturally, as an apple-tree bears apples or a rose-bush roses."[17] Music in this description is very organic, coming up through the roots, a "natural" process. The composer's task is to nourish the seeds, be ready (technically prepared) for the hard work involved, and be free enough to allow the music to flow.

It is not uncommon to find Messiaen in the woods, music paper in hand, notating the unique melodies of his friends in creation. In a very real way creatures like birds are co-creators in his music, since it is their unnotated song which is given new life through the skill of Messiaen's human hand. The human artist pays tribute to the artistry of the winged ones.

> Paul Dukas used to say: "Listen to the birds. They are great masters." I confess not having awaited this advice to admire, analyze and notate some songs of birds. Through the mixture of their songs, birds make extremely refined jumbles of rhythmic pedals. Their

melodic contours, those of merles especially, surpass the human imagination in fantasy. Since they use untempered intervals smaller than the semitone, and as it is ridiculous servilely to copy nature, we are going to give some examples of melodies of the "bird" genre which will be transcription, transformation, and interpretation of the volleys and trills of our little servants of immaterial joy.[18]

... At first to witness to their feelings of love; then to defend their territory; finally, and above all, by pleasure, for birds are far from mechanical creatures; they are artists.[19]

It's probable that in the artistic hierarchy birds are the greatest musicians existing on our planet.[20]

Messiaen offers us one answer to the question: Where does music come from? Underlying his testimony to the artistry of the winged ones is a deep respect for the natural beauty in creation, beauty which might go unnoticed if it were not for the attentive ear of the human who passes by, hears, is captured, and falls in love with this natural musical relative. The music is there, in the examples of birds, in a very audible way; the human takes note, uses, enhances, celebrates, and treasures this gift of the universe.

The elements of music—rhythm, melody, and harmony— are the universe's way of initiating the music-making. We are caught by rhythm, allured by melody, surrounded and expanded by harmony. And yet the music doesn't just happen. Its creation asks a lot of us. Likewise, the global community will not just happen; it, too, will ask a lot of us. So, we shall next explore some attitudes needed for quality music-making, to see how these attitudes are important in our becoming a global community.

Attitudes for Quality Music-Making

As we begin making music together, our work must be characterized by trust. We trust the rhythm of the music not to betray us or cause us to trip. We trust other people to play or sing the rhythm as written so that the music-making venture can proceed. We trust that the melody will not expose us to ridicule or embarrassment. We trust it to reveal to us its richness. And we have faith that those who make harmony with us will support and surround us, not overwhelm or distort our voice. We trust the process of music-making, that with diligence and careful practice we can be part of an exceptionally creative project.

As we trust we also learn to revere the music. We respect the rhythm for its power and learn to have power with the rhythm. We rejoice in the rhythm's ability to catch us and lead us, realizing, however, that uncontrolled rhythm is not helpful or appropriate. As we study the rhythm and work at revealing it, we learn to share in its power, to cooperate with it, but not to give in to it. We become rhythm's partner in co-creating the music. We reverence the great mystery playing before us, but do not belittle its message.

In turn, we bless the melody for its color and its passion. We are happy to contribute our life breath to its re-creation, to sing and play notes off the page and into the air. The melody also has great power to move us and connect us with its cosmic origins. Together we move inside the color and breadth of the harmony, learning also from its power to bind and yet hold distinct, to gather but to respect individual voices.

Can any less trust and reverence be expected from the members of a global community? The basis of community building is friendship and understanding, which in turn require reverence and trust. The global evening news is filled with accounts of mistrust, repeating reasons why we should defend ourselves against others. This mistrust comes from too many years of focusing on how we are all separate and where we all fit in the hierarchy of creation. Music, in partnership with the New Story that science tells, reveals our connectedness and invites us to be more concerned about how we are one, how we are connected. Music can call us back to a reverence for the unique rhythms and special melodies of various cultures, creeds, and creatures, the blessed harmonies of people living well together. Music is an artistic portrayal of what science is asking us to see about how the universe works and how the earth is meant to live.

To make music one must trust and reverence oneself as well as the music. If the player is intimidated by the musical score, the performance may sound more like a struggle for survival or dominance than a dialogue and a "playing" of the instrument. The lesson to learn is to have power with the music, to dialogue with it, to play it, trust it, and reverence it. If the player is afraid of the music, perhaps because it hasn't been learned well enough, the rhythm may begin to have power over the player, to be "out of control." What performer or listener has not experienced moments in music of such loss of control! Being "in control" does not mean beating the music to death, nor does it mean a dry mechan-i cal performance with the music all locked up and unimagina-tive. Having power with the music is enabling—the musician is relaxed but ready, the music seems to flow, not because it is on its own, but because it is well-rehearsed, well-planned, and well-known.

The creation of a global community also cannot be accomplished with some folks having power over the lives of others. Power-with is what music can teach us; this is enabling power, playing power. Leadership in the global civilization must work at enabling people to get into the circle of the earth, the circle of creation. Trust and reverence are the basis for taking up such difficult work.

When the musician sits down to play, one of the inner dialogues that may occur is the one between a feeling of humility, given the task at hand, and an honest sense of personal worth and talent. Humility, in its root sense, means earthiness, being "on the ground." We came from the earth and have an ongoing relationship with the earth. We have our feet firmly grounded, and we realize that the earth is where we belong; it is our home and our mother. We also recognize that whatever we have is a gift to us, that nothing we have has come to us because we earned it or deserved it. In fact, "deserve" is not a very helpful word in discussing life issues; it can be misleading. Life offers us various oppor-tunities. Some may look very bad, but that is not because we deserved them. Others may look very good, and we are more apt to claim those as "deserved." But life happens. To spend our time worrying about whether or not we deserve what life presents is not helpful in responding; in fact, that kind of anxiety may hold us back. Humility allows us to greet life realistically and not to feel defeated by the difficult times it offers, nor to feel smug about what we may have attained. Humility helps keep us honest.

Music is a gift that is not "deserved." Skill and technique in performance must be worked at, and for that work we can take appropriate credit. But musicians know that music is too mysterious and too immense ever to be claimed as someone's own property. It is not "ours" in the sense of belonging to any particular person to the exclusion of any other person. We recognize the power of music to name the themes of life, and we offer our own earthy, earthly bodies as instruments of the music. It is this thought of humility which rises in the musicians's heart when hands touch the keyboard or embrace the violin's neck.

Humility in our music-making reminds us that we are simply not able to determine precisely where the music comes from. It would be very short-sighted, and, in light of the New Cosmological Story, very arrogant, to claim that all the music of the ages originated inside people, without at the same time acknowledging where the insides of people came from. Our earthiness reminds us that all that we are has been shaped by countless ancestors, human as well as non-human. Who could say that there were not many music-makers among them? Our participation in the art of music does not draw us away from the earth so that we can marvel at how wonderful we are; it invites us into the mystery and the music, that we might see how much at home we are in the cosmos.

Participation in this great musical project gives us a companion attitude for humility, namely, an honest sense that we do have unique talents as humans, and that some of us are specially gifted in the art of music-making. A good word to help us in this area is royalty.[21] The universe has waited fifteen billion years for us to make its music, for minds and hearts and hands that can articulate and write down a language for music. This realization gives us great energy and wonder. Human hands are needed to make the note sound, and as the notes are heard we marvel at the music, at the performer, at the artistry and sensitivity of the instrument. This kind of royal feeling is for everyone. And music's theme is that we are earthlings of a special kind. Born of the universe, we have the music of the planets and stars within us. As we release its potential we call others into the song and dance of the universe, we call them to royalty, to celebrating their communion with all creation. The composer is royal, the player or singer is royal, the listener is royal, and all are treated to a royal experience.

The implications for the global civilization fairly jump off the page at us. If all people were awakened to their humility and their royal personhood, all kinds of things could happen. Governments that oppress, class systems and dead institutions that cling to ladder-models of reality would lose their power to allure people or control them. As the deeper human values of communion and personal worth are uncovered and taught, as trust in each other and the universe grows and expands, people of all places would be able to realize that no human person is more royal than another and that all of us belong in the circling music of creation.

Trust and reverence are attitudes necessary for entering the music-making. Once we begin, we need humility and a royal sense of self to proceed. Next we need hard work, practice, discipline, and cooperation.

To practice the music is not to mechanically repeat again and again the patterns of the printed page, but to learn the music, to dialogue with it, to treasure its beauty, to understand how it works, and yet to be continually surprised by its richness and intrigued by its mystery. It is the music itself that provides the discipline, the teaching, the demands needed for performance.

As an example, let us consider a difficult passage in a piece of music. The player discovers the passage in first reading the music. Perhaps he or she may be puzzled by it and wonder what it is doing there! As the player/practicer works at the passage, it will reveal itself gradually. The inner structure of the passage as well as its place in the context of a larger section must be scrutinized. The difficulty of the

39

passage may intimidate the player. Patient and slow work will open up the musical mystery and break down the fear, replacing it with knowledge and pleasure. The passage will gradually be learned (by the brain or by the fingers). The most facile performance of this piece of music will be accomplished not when the player feels intimidated by the difficulty of the passage (the music has power over me) nor when the player feels a smug satisfaction that the passage is "not really that hard" (I now have power over music), but when the player and the music become partners toward the goal of music-making, when they share the power of the music together.

To learn the music the fingers must be ready, available to the demands of the music. The head and heart must focus and concentrate, giving their energies to the musical task. The ear must hear, correct, critique, particularly in the practice sessions while the performer is working and testing. One of the hardest disciplines for many players is that of listening to themselves as they play. The instrument itself may also require new disciplines—some keyboards are stiffer than others, some strings warmer than others. The best instruments are all unique and have their own special character. The player must be ready to adapt to the instrument to make music with it. Some instruments will feel ready and willing in the hands of the performer, "friendly" you might say. Others may put a person off by their inaccessible or stubborn feel. Some instruments need time to settle in: a ten-year-old pipe organ is still very new. The performer approaches a new instrument with excitement and perhaps some trepidation. Some instruments are very revealing of the player's inadequacies. A get-acquainted period is necessary—time for the player to try the instrument and the instrument to try the player. Again the desired result is the player's feeling power with the instrument, not over it or under it, but with it. The power is enabling power, the magic for music-making.

When one is part of an assembly of music-makers, another theme of discipline is that of working with others, cooperating with them and with the conductor. This may take hours of practice time together, in addition to the practice time of the individual players. Even alone, however, the ensemble musician is working at the group project. For if a player arrives unrehearsed, "unpracticed," the ability of the whole group to make music will be diminished. A player's failure to respond to the conductor's direction, for example, will frustrate the conductor as well as the other players. To cooperate—to work with and feel power with—to make music with—is also to feel responsibility and ownership for the project. In this kind of ownership the music is not "mine" as opposed to "yours" but the more cooperative "ours." The symphony is ours to play, the cantata is ours to sing. It may also "belong" to others who know it and perform it as well. But in this special performance we own it and have power with it. We play or sing it from our heart, which is also the heart of the universe.

The musical score teaches and disciplines us, the particular instrument may ask special skill of us, and the performing group needs our cooperation. We offer our private practice time to the common time of the group. And our private practice time is shaped by the needs of the assembly who will make the music. So we have many teachers. In the best performance the practice and discipline are not apparent— the observers/listeners do not notice them, although they may be indirectly aware that excellence in performance is not easily attained. What is noticed is a flow in the music, a rapport among the musicians, a cooperation which energizes and animates the whole performance.

Once again we ask: Can these attitudes of discipline and cooperation be applied to our global project? Even a very young musician can tell you that one cannot expect to play without practice. Only day-to-day, consistent, and disciplined time with the voice or the instrument will result in quality music-making. It would be foolish to expect a grand performance when we have not practiced. Isn't it true, though, that we practice selfishness and self-centeredness, pride and ambition, and then expect to live in a cooperative and peaceful world? Nations worry only for themselves, feed themselves, protect themselves, arm themselves, boast of their wealth, and then expect to live as one world with other nations who don't have enough food or resources to survive. Music reveals the flaw: what we want to perform, to "happen," we must practice. We must practice generosity, compassion, and justice daily, until we learn them well, "by heart" the musician would say, so that these qualities can flow from us as the music of the symphony flows from the players. Then we can bring our own practice to the larger human venture, so that this community can practice being the global civilization it wishes to become. As the musician practices, the music is already being made, becoming a reality. As people practice being global in their attitudes, the vision of a world civilization is already becoming real.

We cannot wait for others to make a world community for us. The players cannot expect anyone else to practice for them, or cover for their lack of practice. This brings us to an additional question: What motivates the musician to work so hard? And what will motivate us to work as hard at our global project? The musician who is enthralled with the beauty of the music understands why hard study and practice are necessary. Even in the long hours of solo practice, the vision of the symphony is present with the musician. There is also enjoyment in the communal experience of music-making: the breathing and bowing, playing and singing together. There is a very real sense of a worthwhile contribution to a living work of art, to the shaping of themes and melodies and the revelation and presentation of the notes on the printed page, in this unique musical moment.

What if people were to become excited about the beauty of their global adventure? What if they could envision the wonder of the universe in the same way that a violinist practicing in her music room envisions (hears) the whole orchestra playing? This new context would give us strength to see that what may seem small and unrelated individual activities of global awareness are an important part of the practicing of the world we are becoming. We see/hear our daily activities played out within the scope of a larger activity—the global project. As the single violinist in the music room understands the importance of practice for the successful performance of the symphony, so we see our daily practice of justice to be crucial to the growth of justice on our planet. As the solo player sees that his practice strengthens the assembly of musicians and their music, so the individual person knows that just deeds strengthen a just civilization on its way to becoming a reality. If the musician doesn't practice, that irresponsibility affects the whole project. Other musicians may call delinquent players to account. Isn't our lack of practicing for this global community also irresponsible and debilitating for the community? Who will call us to accountability for a lack of "practice," for our irresponsibility and narrowness of vision? Why not musicians?

> ...I know that there are those who believe artists should live in an ivory tower, removed from the struggles and suffering of their fellow men. That is a concept to which I have never been able to suscribe. An affront to human dignity is an affront to me; and to protest injustice is a matter of conscience. Are human rights of less importance to an artist than to other men? Does being an artist exempt one from his responsibilities as a man? If anything, the artist has a particular responsibility, because he has been granted special sensitivities and perceptions, and because his voice may be heard when other voices are not. Who, indeed, should be more concerned than the artist with the defense of liberty and free inquiry, which are essential to his very creativity?[22]

This excerpt from the memoirs of Pablo Casals is an inspiring challenge to musicians who are content not to be involved with the wider realm of society and culture. His self-imposed exile from his Catalonian homeland after the Spanish Civil War stands even now, thirteen years after his death, as a vibrant and relevant witness to the trust, reverence, and sense of royalty which should characterize the artistic venture. More a world citizen than a national patriot, Casals sought to break through political and nationalistic barriers by making music, a universe of music.

We have noted that music teaches us the importance of disciplined practice. The goal of practice time is to "learn" the music, not only the progression of notes across the page, but also the secrets of what makes the music work. Likewise, in our global civilization, practice must be disciplined so that precious time is not wasted. It is the vision that disciplines us, that requires our careful and respectful attention, that motivates us to keep practicing, even when the music of a just and peaceful planet seems to elude us.

Even as the musicians are learning the notes, something else is happening: they are being creative with, or co-creative with, the music. The music is silent on the page until the notes are played or sung. But each time they are played or sung they will sound different. Each note, each time, is re-creative. There are a hundred things that could change: the pressure of the bow on the strings, the embouchure of lips meeting the trumpet, the strike of the mallet on the kettledrum. Added to these possible differences is the conscious creativity of the musician in playing, often called "interpretation." The players imagine other sounds, other ways to sound the note, and are creative with their skill and talents. Sometimes hours can be spent in working through problems of interpretation. Research and study are helpful, but often also confusing. Ultimately this musician must use all the resources at hand and create; this conductor must raise the baton and begin again.

Perhaps never before in our planetary history have imagination and creativity been so critical. It is the process of imagining the whole symphony which gives the composer courage to take pen in hand and write the first note. It is the imagining of the same symphony which encourages the cello player to learn the part. It will be the imagining of a global civilization which will call us out of complacency and our anthropocentric (human-centered) world view to begin to act creatively to build a future which values all life.

As noted earlier, the Hebrew book of Genesis tells us that we are made in the image of a very creative God. Image has the same root as imagine, and also imitate. If we are God's images, we must imitate our Creator by doing what God does. What God does is create. Our task is further spelled out in our stewardship role as two-legged caretakers of the earth and its goodness. In the musical agenda a performance date often looms on the horizon, a point when the musicians will be accountable for their talent and their practice. That date becomes the focus of energy and time, so that at the moment of performance the players or singers will be most ready with the music. The global civilization has no performance date, although "the day" may be upon us at any moment. It can be a day of vast destruction or a day or marvelous creativity. Are we ready? Are we getting ready? Are we even practicing?

Our planet is at a critical point. We must be creative about shaping our future, or there will be no future. Old solutions simply won't work any more. Nationalistic decision-making is not broad enough; care of just our own is not only unfriendly, it is not wise. We must imagine the kind of earth we want to hand to our descendants, for we are the co-creators of the future. As with music, we need to hear the theme song of a global community so that its tune will allure us and motivate us to make it happen.

Over and over again we have noticed that it is the vision of the symphony which motivates the solo player to keep practicing. (There doesn't seem to be an audio-equivalent for this meaning of the sighted word vision.) When the symphony is performed, how do players as well as listeners experience it? It is certainly not static or flat space, not inanimate, but somehow alive, multidimensional. It is not a jumble of parts each begging for our attention, playing away without reference to each other (unless that is the intention of the composer). Could not one way to describe symphony be to call it a living organism?

By definition, an organism has parts which are interdependent, each part having a specific function in relation to the working of the whole. The organism is about the carrying on of life. These characteristics can be seen in music, and are more helpful in understanding it than a mechanical metaphor: music as a machine with all parts doing their work. The parts played by various instrumentalists are interdependent, and their relationship is shaped by the contour of the whole piece. But for the symphony to live and breathe, the parts must give conscious attention to this relationship (trust, reverence, humility, and the like). This is much more than a mechanical event. The players live and breathe, the instruments cooperate, the music is played, and the song of the universe is heard again.

In a global community the parts (countries, nations, and so on) are also interdependent, related, and dialoguing with the whole to understand this relationship. They must give conscious attention to this cooperation for the organism which is our planet to live well. It is possible to play a symphony dryly, unimaginatively, even in a toiling way. But that is not making music. There needs to be juice in the playing, flow in the music. For the global civilization to be alive it also must be lived imaginatively, and that means with life and enthusiasm. Hildegard would say:

> It is this vigor that hugs the world:
> warming, moistening, firming, greening.
>
> This is so that all creatures
> might germinate and grow. [23]

The kind of enthusiasm that energizes the players of the symphony and keeps an organism growing and glowing must also characterize the population of the planetary community. We need imagination and fertile hearts which will allow us to move and change and accept new seedlings among us.

Who makes the music? Where does it come from? Who makes community? Where does it come from?

Although the exact origins of the art of music are uncertain, it is clear that there are some people who are more musical than others. There are people who can hear music before it is written down, and there are people who can look at the written notes and hear their sounds. Composers and musicians can hear different ways of playing and singing the same music, and are sensitive to the colors and shapes of sounds in a way that astounds the less musical ear. Because of their unique gifts, the people whom we call "musicians" already have within them some tendency toward making music. We may say that the music is already "in them," waiting to come out through an instrument or through the human voice. In this sense the musicians re-create the music, give shape and form and texture to something intangible, so that it can be heard and enjoyed by others.

A composer does this in a very creative way, by putting the sounds and silence together in a particular way, resulting in a "new" piece. This new piece is able to be identified as a unique work, although it may have themes or harmonies that remind the listener of other music. In the history of music (as in the visual arts) we come to recognize various styles or schools: Wagnerian harmony, French organ masses, English anthems. Members of the school may work with a particular sound, color, or musical idea so that their music sounds related. Composers borrow forms like sonata or fugue and infuse them with their own creativity. And yet we sense how deeply those writers are related, how cleverly they each use the basic musical material at their disposal (scales and keys), how eagerly they cooperate with the co-creative musical activity of the universe.

The player or singer who learns a new piece is also creative, and co-creative with the composer. Both people are cooperating with something inside them, some musical seed which germinates and grows and blossoms. When the first tender musical shoots are noticed, the young seedling finds itself transplanted firmly on the piano bench or poised with violin or flute in hand. The teaching and the study—the cultivation—begins. Without this attention and affirmation the musical seed will not grow. We would grieve that a great opportunity had been missed and that the universe had been deprived of some great music-making. The seed image for music reminds us that music is alive, organic, fragile, needing care and nourishment. Because it is organic, music does not develop in a person overnight. Patience and resilience are needed, just as much as for the young plant hopeful of bearing fruit.

If music is a seed planted within us, is there a comparable seed for the global civilization? Is there something in us as potent as the musical seed, something that wants to germinate and grow into a broader project than individual survival? We would not hear the symphony if the composer did not work at writing it and the instrumentalist work at learning it. Can we arrive at a global civilization if the seeds of that project are not given space and nourishment to grow in us?

Here the Christian tradition offers us a helpful image: the Trinitarian God: Creator, Redeemer, and Spirit. God is community. If we are the image of God, is not this mysteriously communal tendency a God-given seed within us, woven into every fiber in our bodies, every spiral of DNA?

> The seed of God is in us.
>   Now
>   the seed of a pear tree
>   grows into a pear tree;
>   and a hazel seed
>   grows into a hazel tree;
> a seed of God
>   grows into
>   God. [24]

The seed image is helpful to us in thinking about musicians and how music is in them. It is also helpful when thinking about our global community. If God is three persons and the seed of God is in us, what can it mean that we are growing into God? Are we not communal in our deepest reality, in being the image and imitators of God? The seed of music must be nourished if music is to be heard. The seed of God in each of us must be watered, kept moist and green, if it is to grow. The seeds of global living must also be cultivated if we are to "grow up" into the universe's vision for us. Our tendency toward community, sharing, and circling together must be tended. For those in whom the gift of making connections or revealing connections is especially present, affirmation and support are important. How do we nourish our leaders? What kind of training do we give them? Maybe we should require them all to play in a symphony orchestra for a year.

Striving to do our best is appropriate both in music-making and in global living. Our mistake usually comes in thinking that we do our best by putting others down, incapacitating them or debilitating them. The pleasure of performing well is overshadowed by the joy of defeating. Again, music reveals the flaw in our thinking: you can't make music by putting down the other players in the symphony. Even if you are the first chair in the violin section! In fact, if you are the first chair, you have a greater responsibility for how the players work together, how they make music together, rather than how they compete. The symphony is living and the parts are interdependent. The wind instruments do not consider that they win when they get to play the melody. This kind of language (winning or losing) does not fit the musical art. The winds would say that everyone wins when the music is made, when the sections work together, when the whole symphony lives and breathes and engages both players and listeners in a musical mystical event.

Would that the language of competition, the aim to win or lose, were as inappropriate in our global living! Would that we could work for laws where everyone wins, where everyone is pleased to be a part of the human project, where children look forward to growing up into being leaders in a healthy community instead of committing suicide! But what about the seeds of community in our children? Are they nourished at all?

> And what do we teach our children in school? We teach them that two and two make four, and that Paris is the capital of France. When will we also teach them what they are? We should say to each of them: Do you know what you are? You are a marvel! You are unique! In all of the world there is no other child exactly like you. In all the millions of years that have passed there has never been another child like you. And look at your body— what a wonder it is! your legs, your arms, your cunning fingers, the way you move! You may become a Shakespeare, a Michelangelo, a Beethoven. You have the capacity for anything. Yes, you are a marvel. And when you grow up, can you then harm another who is, like you, a marvel? You must cherish one another. You must work—we all must work—to make this world worthy of its children.[25]

What has been proposed is this first section is that music-making is rich in images that are helpful when we think of our task in the universe, particularly as citizens of the global community we call Earth. The New Story of the Cosmos may at first overwhelm us, and we may be unsure about how or whether to respond to its invitation. Music can teach us how to respond, how to go about being worthy creatures of the planet.

For the power of the images of music to be released however, two things must happen. 1. People need to be reawakened to what music proposes, what its power is, what a special gift of the universe it is, and how music is for everyone. 2. Musicians themselves must be reawakened to what the music proposes, be responsible for its power and its message, and be ready for their task as global artists, as artists of the universe.

Music can teach us—teach our presidents and dictators, teach our scientists and our theologians, teach those who are oppressed and suppressed, teach our children. It can but it needs the willing bodies of those whose special talent it is to hear how alluring music is, how powerful it is, how willing to be released into the universe to re-echo the Creator's original Song.

We have proposed that music is in the universe, in the air, so to speak. In the next section we will look more closely at how the earth and its elements help us and teach us in the music-making process, and how human words that speak universal truths can now expand and become the song of the universe.

PART II

We Sing with the Earth
Discovering Our Cosmic
Connections

Introduction

Air

Air moves us,
Fire transforms us,
Water shapes us,
Earth heals us,
And the balance of the wheel
goes round and round,
the balance of the wheel
goes round.
Starhawk[1]

Many primal religions celebrated the four elements: air, fire, water, and earth. These elements are gifts of the earth which has unique and origin-al traits that are so helpful in nourishing us. And since music is our special interest, we shall explore how the four elements are present in our music-making and how they are an invitation into the singing and dancing of the universe. We reflect with the elements of the earth to discover how they cooperate with us in the music-making and in our cosmic connecting.

3

The Power of the Elements of the Earth

Air

I add my breath to
your breath
That our days may
be long on the Earth
That the days of our
people may be long
That we may be one person
That we may finish
our roads together
May my father bless
you with life
May our Life Path be
fulfilled.

—A Native American Song[1]

Hearing this native American song, we may want to reflect on the question: Who is "I" in the song? Who is the singer? From the text it seems likely that "I" is a parent, or perhaps any tribal member, and that the song is one of communion or commitment, as for a marriage ritual. According to our understanding of the cosmos, the earth has engendered the human community, including making choices about the air that is our breath, so that the earth might be singing "I add my breath to your breath that our days may be long here..." This way of hearing the song gives a whole new depth to the word ecology. It challenges us to look at ecology as a way of loving and caring for the earth because it is our mother, our womb, our teacher, and source of wisdom. Ecology, then, is a result of our deep sense of communion with the earth and all its creatures, including the human family.

Other singers of this song might be the great religious figures of the ages. The text offers a theology remarkably similar to that of many of the sayings of Jesus Christ, particularly as recorded in the Gospel of John (see especially the last discourse, John 14:1-4; 15:9-12 or 17:20-23). Again we can wonder where the song comes from, where the inspiration for such universe-al singing is born. The best songs, it seems, are the ones that everyone can sing including non-two-legged creatures, even the universe itself.

The starting place for this song is the sharing of the breath of life. It is reminiscent of the Hebrew account of the creation of the human species as recorded in the second chapter of Genesis. In this story God is depicted as breathing into the clay form and the human is "born." The air is not only personal life breath, but the spark of the divine life in us. Breathing is our survival use of air, but because of its origin, our survival takes on cosmic significance. We receive the breath of life from the Creator of the universe, so that every breath we take is a remembering, a thanksgiving, a celebration of that origin. It is also of communal importance, since air is also for exchange and interdependence. Plants take in carbon dioxide and release oxygen. Humans return the favor. The trading of air is built into the universe, orchestrated for us by the universe, celebrated in its rhythms of life.

Perhaps this is why a common preparation for meditation is attention to our breathing, not even necessarily "deep breathing," but simply recollection, awareness of our personal rhythm of air movement. Attention to this air flow helps to "open up" our inside space to allow for a freer flow of consciousness. There is more space inside us, more room for meditation to happen. Our insides are cleared out, "purified" with our own life (divine) breath. Thus breathing becomes a kind of fasting, a discipline for spiritual growth, a means toward centering.

Attention to breathing is also an important part of the healing process. By sending air through the part of the body in need of healing, we release its special energy, we "open up" the area that tends to constrict in the tension of pain. We allow the life-giving nature of the air to caress and ease the soreness or tightness. Yoga-like breathing techniques are useful for the relaxation of weary muscles as well as the clearing of one's head after a long day. Recent "discoveries" of the importance of rhythmic breathing in the birth process return us to the wisdom of primal people and highlight the significance of working with the gifts we already have for healing, for cooperating with our "natural" processes.

This opening up and connecting character of breathing, this free-flowing gift of air, reveals new things about our music-making. Music is made, literally, on air. Just as our life breath subtly pours through our body cells, so music seems to flow around in us. We "hear" it with our ears, and yet we feel it and sometimes see it, perhaps (if we are very imaginative) even smell and taste it. There are two sides to this story: the side of the music-maker and the side of the music-hearer. We already have noted the magnificent and very personal gift which is made when someone's life breath is given in song or in playing an instrument. The music is made with life breath, which is of divine and cosmic origin, and yet which is very intimate to the music-maker. Releasing this life breath in song is therefore a cosmic event. Each time music is made, a basic gift of the universe is acknowledged and celebrated, and a person—no matter how distant, how alone, how unnoticed—is using cosmic air.

Part of the puzzle of this way of thinking about music is that air is not something tangible (unless it is wind, which we shall discuss shortly). The only time we see air is when we have polluted it so badly that it becomes visible. And yet even then we are not seeing air but what is in the air. We don't smell air itself, although it is a wonderful carrier of smells. We may become so accustomed to smelly air that fresh air nearly knocks us out. Our culture does not readily acknowledge or celebrate things that we can't see. And yet we use air all the time: our airplanes climb on it, kites fly on it, balloons float in it, hawks soar on it, snowflakes dance in it. Music is an opportunity for us to use air well, to play with it and on it, to enjoy it as does the hawk or the kite.

Because air is invisible and intangible we may take its friendliness for granted. We are more likely to be concerned about things that we see. Because of our short-sightedness in this regard, elements which have come to us as life-givers can become deadly. A practical example has to do with insects. We see bugs in our house and they annoy us. So we kill them with chemicals, whose effect (except for the dead bugs) we cannot see. It is quite possible that the chemicals may be much more harmful to us than the bugs, but we don't "see" that, at least not immediately. Our shortsightedness becomes a trap for us. We abuse the air and our own breathing system as we pollute our space with chemicals and sprays. This abuse ultimately affects the great air surrounding the earth. The ozone which has been our friend is being destroyed. And the sun who has been an original friend has become hurtful to us as rays which are harmful begin to pour through holes we have poked in our atmospheric blanket.

Two other aspects of air's presence among us deserve attention here. The first is the aspect of space. We often refer to "empty space," meaning that no thing is there (except the air, which we cannot see and so tend not to count). The empty space is valuable, however, in the appropriate arrangement of things. In a room, for example, not enough space between objects makes us feel crowded out, not welcome. A space for human living should invite us in, make us feel that we belong in the space rather than feel cramped in it. Does a church look better empty than full? Does it get cluttered when people arrive? Does the furniture welcome us, reflect what we are about? Who is the space for anyway?

In our house we may fill up room space, clutter it with things so that people who venture there feel they can't move. We can clutter our personal space in the same way, so that our lives are filled up with things rather than being free and flexible for us. What are the things in our space? Do they control our day, determine its shape? Or is there room for the unexpected, the stranger, the surprise? What is the quality of our personal space? What is in the air around us? Our air can be quiet or cluttered with noise. It can also be used for meaningful sound—music, or good conversation, or just natural sounds. Noise in our air is like too much furniture in the room. And yet our aural sense seems to be able to take much more clutter than our visual. We grow accustomed to elevators with music and beaches with radios, frequently not even realizing the assault on our ears and on our personal air space. We suffer from air pollution because of the dirt there but also because of the noise there.

Perhaps this pollution of our space (both visually and aurally) can be treated with art, since the appropriate use of sound and silence, as well as the placement of objects in the painting or the choice of colors in the weaving, can teach us about the importance of space. In particular, Oriental art, which understands the value of space and understatement, can be healing for our eyes. We are invited into the space of the picture. In other styles, large open canvasses and asymmetrical designs can challenge our thinking about the importance of space and how much breathing room we need to survive and live well.

A second expression of air that interests us is wind.

> ...Creation supplies us with only two kinds of things: necessities and extras. Sunlight, air, water, food, shelter—these are among the bare necessities. With them we can exist. But moonlight and starlight are distinctly extras; so are music, the perfumes, flowers. The wind is perhaps a necessity; but the song that it croons through the morning pines is a different thing.[2]

Just in case we are tempted to ignore air or to trivialize it, the universe sends us wind. Wind delights us, energizes us, sweeps us away. It can storm and rage around us and even destroy us or the things we have made. It cleanses and refreshes, it bends and shapes, it tosses trees and blows dandelions apart, sending their seed all over our lawns. Its power can be harnessed and helping or wild and fearful. Like still air, wind cannot be seen (unless it becomes a tornado), but its presence is noted by its activity. Like air and music, wind envelops and embraces us without our even asking.

Air is essential to our music-making, since music is made "on air." It is another partner with the player, the instrument, the composer, the score, the listener. Air is the enabler, for without air the music could not be heard. Some instruments even take their name—"wind"—from air. Players of these instruments make a wind to produce the musical sound. There are many variations in the mechanics of those instruments: no reed, a single reed, a double reed, all relying on air and its unique characteristics to make sound.

Musicians, then, should be very concerned about air quality, for eventually its pollution will affect our music-making. Imagine sixty players coughing their way through a Beethoven symphony or a soloist sneezing and wheezing through a flute sonata. Haydn made a good point in his so-called "Farewell" Symphony. In 1772 the musicians were working at the country palace of Prince Nicolaus at Eszterháza. They had been kept away from home and family for much too long, and so they prepared a musical statement. During the symphony's last movement each player or a small group of players blew out their candles, gathered their instruments and left, until there was no one left to play. The prince got the idea and recessed the musicians. If musicians in this day are tired of breathing dirty air and trying to make good music with it, perhaps a "Clean Air" symphony needs to be written. In this rendition player by player could don gas masks until the music (like other earth creatures) gradually chokes to death.

The air is our friend, but we have not always acted as friend to the air. Before it is too late (and some are saying that it already is too late) we must reverse our polluting habits and celebrate the air which is our life. I add my breath to your breath, and my music to your music, that our days may be long on the earth.

We can rise with the fire of free-dom___

Truth is a fire that burns our chains. And we can

stop the fires of des----truc--tion___

Heal-ing is a fire run-nin' through our veins

This contemporary chant[3], written as part of a blockade at Livermore Laboratories which took place on 2 February 1982, expresses some very primal wisdom about fire. In pre-Christian religions, the symbol of fire rules "energy, spirit, heat, flame, blood, sap, life, will, healing and destroying, purification, bonfires, hearthfires, candle flames, sun, deserts, volcanoes, eruptions, explosions."[4] This particular chant plays with positive and negative aspects of fire: it is searing, purifying, healing, or destructive and frightening. The "fire of freedom" is the energizing spirit that catches those who are engaged in breaking through oppression and injustice. This is a huge flame that cannot be quenched. Even if temporarily doused, it smolders quietly in the hearts of those who have seen the vision of freedom. Recognizing the "truth" of our identity as creatures of the cosmos, we allow that fire to burn away what holds us in bondage. This purifying action of fire is also strengthening; gold and silver are tested and purified in the smith's fire.

Not all of fire's attributes are constructive, however. Used unwisely or without care, fire can be destructive of creation and burn "out of control." Harnessed, it is power for healing and warming, excellent for cooking and snuggling by, or singing songs around. This special gift of Earth is also a unique gift, since fire has not been found anywhere else in the universe.

Of all the planets we know about, fire exists only on Earth. Perhaps the day will come when we discover another planet where fire can exist. That would be a stupendous event. We would feel a special affection for such a world. We would adopt it as a sister planet, as cities adopt sister cities. But until that day comes, we have the situation—awesome and amazing—of knowing that a single planet in the known universe creates fire, and that is Earth.[5]

Ignited by lightning from the universe, stolen from the gods, erupting from the center of the earth, fire evokes mystery and power, visions and wisdom. The story of Moses and the burning bush begins a long Hebrew tradition of fire revelatory of divine presence (see Exodus 3; 13:21-22; 40:38 or Numbers 9:15 or Psalm 78:14). This tradition extends into the Christian Testament, with the disciples' reception of the Holy Spirit, symbolized by tongues of flame above their heads. This fire burns the chains of fear and transforms the disciples in an otherwise unaccountable way to proclaim the gospel of Jesus Christ (see Acts 2).

Christian ritual's use of fire occurs most commonly in candle lighting. Candles are used for ceremony (in processions, at Mass), as a sign of presence (sanctuary light), for vigil in prayer (votive candles), as a symbol of participation in the cosmic light of Christ (baptismal candles). One of the most dramatic uses of this primal earth gift is the kindling of the new fire at the Christian Easter Vigil. The ritual book (sacramentary) prescribes that the "entire celebration of the Easter Vigil takes place at night. It should not begin before nightfall; it should end before daybreak Sunday."[6] It also indicates that the fire should be "large." Attention to these ritual prescriptions means helping to unfold the power of the fire image. The gathering space should be very dark so that the fire is stunning. The blaze should be large enough to impress us with its elementary power. Even though the accompanying prayer indicates that the fire is to remind us of the light of Christ conquering death, we may reach back further than that, remembering that Christ's fire-light burns brightly in the line of the scriptural tradition of fire as sign of presence. We might even remember that initial burst of Creator-fire that began all the fire we now know. This does not diminish the light of Christ, but strengthens its universal significance. The song which concludes the Easter Vigil fire ritual, the Exsultet, has many cosmic themes: "Rejoice, heavenly powers, sing choirs of angels... Rejoice, O earth, in shining splendor, radiant in the brightness of your king... Let it (this flame) mingle with the lights of heaven and continue bravely burning." This text expands our vision outward to all the lights of heavenly space, and backward to the first morning star, the primal fire of the first hundredth of a creation second.

It is this primal fire of which the mystic Hildegard writes.

> God says:
> I am the supreme fire;
> not deadly, but rather,
> enkindling every spark of life. [7]

> I, the fiery life of divine wisdom,
> I ignite the beauty of the plains,
> I sparkle the water,
> I burn in the sun
>   and the moon,
>   and the stars.
> With wisdom I order ALL rightly.
> Above ALL I determine truth. [8]

It is also the fire of which a contemporary theologian speaks.

> In the beginning was *power*, intelligent, loving, energizing. In the beginning was the *word*, supremely capable of mastering and moulding whatever might come into being in the world of matter. In the beginning there were not coldness and darkness: there was *fire*. This is the truth. [9]

What can fire teach about music-making? Are there characteristics of fire which are akin to those of music? Fire's enlivening, inspiring power may be like the creative and visionary energy that sparks our music-making, as when a composer burns to get the notes onto the paper, or when a performer is said to play with "fire" and energy. Music's power for engaging, its ability to catch us, is like the spreading potential of fire. And, like fire, music that is shared is not diminished but glows even more brightly.

To test this analogy further, let us return to Starhawk's fire chant and substitute the word "music" where we have sung "fire." The song would begin:

We can rise with the music of freedom.

Passion-filled songs that have risen from the hearts of oppressed people have become storehouses of energy for them and for others in bondage. Both the lyrics and the music of such songs become a bonding force and a call to prophecy. Like the tongues of fire above the disciples' heads, this fire-music transforms its singers in an unaccountable way. They are able to be inspired and challenged by the searing honesty of the music. They catch its message as its movement catches them.

Truth is the music that burns our chains.

The truth of the music can be its universe-al message, a message not bound by national lines or racial differences. At the same time, songs of nationalism and competition can be tools of separatism and even war-making. These manipulative possibilities threaten more clearly when we try the third phrase.

We can stop the music of destruction.

This phrase may jar us. How could there be music of destruction? Does our analogy fall apart here?

Unfortunately there have been times when music has been used for separation rather than communion. Examples, even in recent history, are all too plentiful: the theme from Beethoven's Fifth Symphony became the "v" for victory motif for the allies in World War II; the band played "Don't cry for me Argentina" when the British soldiers left for the Falkland Islands War. The underlying militaristic themes of too many Christian hymns raise serious questions about their use in the "communion" of worship. Arguments continue across the country, and around the world, about the lyrics of rock songs, not to mention the effect of their music or their assault on our air space.

To ignore the other side of the power of music would be naive, just as it would be silly to pretend that fire cannot be destructive. Planning music for ritual often feels like playing with fire. Music can be manipulative, can stir people, rouse them, bond them, move them, without necessarily being backed by a life-giving motive. Music is certainly not inherently destructive. Yet if its power is not reckoned with it also can get "out of control." Musicians of integrity must challenge abuses of music's power just as they must stand against the misuse of other earth powers. It seems incongruous that musicians can play together a piece of music that is meant to divide and rouse to war. The music-making activity itself requires mutual respect and cooperation; this does not mean the player is passive or unreflective. But we can ignore the worthy attitude which music asks us to have, and allow it also to be distorted and destructive. Waking up to what a contradiction is present in this kind of music-making will help us to stand against it. What if they gave a war and nobody came? What if they wrote war music and no musicians would play it? The final line of the song offers a corrective to these destructive possibilities:

Healing is the music running through our veins.

Perhaps this line appeals most to our poetic and cosmic souls. Healing runs through us like music, breathing and singing in us, purifying and dancing in us—our individual bodies, our corporate body, the body of the earth, the body of the universe. This fire transforms us as it frees us, releasing our energy for restoration and healing.

Water

Water is the most complex and, besides air, the most important substance of life on earth. Its quality is the environmental indicator par excellence... Water is not consumed but borrowed—and borrowed things should be returned in their original condition. [10]

"Borrow" is an interesting word to use as expressing our relationship to all the earth elements. For Native Americans it is ludicrous to think that any individual could own land— the land is for the people, all the people. How much more strange to try to own the ever-flowing water. As soon as water escapes its container it will move wherever it pleases. Like fire and wind, water has great power that can turn destructive if not respected and treasured. Too often we minimize water's meaning, or trivialize its importance in our lives—"it's only water!" Recovering the power of water as a ritual symbol will help to open up its cleansing, nourishing and birthing talents.

Many primal people recognized the original womb of water.

> Everything was water, water as far as the eye could see. But above the water rose the tree Teri-Ramula. As time passed a worm was born in the tree and it began to eat the wood. The dust fell into the water year after year, until slowly the world was formed. [11]

> In the beginning one of the gods of heaven stirred the chaotic waters with his staff. When he raised the staff muddy foam dripped down from it, this expanded and thickened until it formed the islands of Japan... [12]

> In the beginning there was only darkness everywhere— darkness and water. And the darkness gathered thick in places; out of one of the places where the darkness had crowded there came forth a man. This man wandered through the darkness until he began to think; then he knew himself and that he was a man. He knew that he was there for some purpose. [13]

> The Virgin of the Air descends into the sea, where she is fertilized by the winds and waves and becomes the Water-Mother. A teal builds its nest on her knee, and lays eggs. The eggs fall from the nest and break, but the fragments form the earth, sky, sun, moon and clouds. [14]

The Hebrew Scriptures are filled with water stories, the first found in the second verse of the first chapter of Genesis, where God's spirit is hovering over the already-present water. Shortly the division of waters occurs, above and below the vault, and then the separation of water from land. Later the water is bid to teem with living creatures and so becomes (as science now verifies) a great birthing ocean.

In a second Genesis story water is not so creative of life. When Noah and his family escape in the ark, the earth and all living things are engulfed and destroyed. We are faced with earth's violence, its vengeance for disrespectful treatment of its gifts. This flooding still occasionally goes unchecked. Its speed and power defy human logic or imagination, and embarrass our attempts at control. Like air and fire, water is an important ally, but an ally that deserves our respectful attention, for it can also harm us.

The Christian use of water in the baptismal ritual offers several themes. Immersion in water is a sign of letting go of a past way of life and being converted to a new one, a returning to the womb, in a sense, to renew one's life commitment. It is also an initiation into a community, a community whose members are baptismally naked before each other. This radical sense of equality and communion are hallmarks of those who have been "baptized in Christ." Finally (and historically later in the development of the theology of Christian baptism) the water has a cleansing effect, a washing away of sin, a purification reminiscent of the letting go and rebirth images. The rebirth in baptism is so powerful that it opens up for the believer a sharing in eternal life.

> Are you aware that we who were baptized into Christ Jesus were baptized into his death? Through baptism into his death we were buried with him, so that, just as Christ was raised from the dead by the glory of the Father, we too might live a new life. If we have been united with him through likeness to his death, so shall we be united with him through a like resurrection. [15]

It is noteworthy that this portion of the sixth chapter of Romans is offered in the Roman Lectionary both for services of Christian initiation and Christian burial. On both occasions the water becomes the womb of life, the place where water surrounds and envelops us, urging us, carrying us into new life.

A contemporary story indicates another critical water-gift: nourishment for life and symbol of life continuing. Women attending the 1985 United Nations Conference on Women in Nairobi, Kenya, heard of a great project being carried on by native women outside the city. When observers arrived, they found the women digging a hole in the dry, drought-stricken earth. They were using small implements, whatever was at hand for digging. And they were singing. When asked about the purpose and value of this seemingly small gesture, the women told of their frustration during the months of drought and their anger at not being able to do anything. Out of their recycled anger came the project: to dig a hole to gather the rain when it finally would come. Their song was a mixture of confidence, hope, and incredible trust that the earth would respond to this project. Their music-making was more than a distraction from the drudgery of their labor; it was part of the digging, part of the praying, part of the movement toward the accomplishment not only of the great hole, but also of the great rain. Their song, born of the earth, returns to the earth, and speaks of and for the earth's own desire for moistening and growing power. We are left with the question: How important to the rain's coming was the raising of the song?

Water has been recognized as revelatory of divine providence (see Exodus 17 and John 4) and therefore presence. Once again Hildegard speaks.

> The soul that is full of wisdom
> is saturated with the spray of
> a bubbling fountain—God himself.[16]

This divinely poured water keeps us moist and green so that we can grow. Rain is another aspect of this nourishing water. Like air, the rain has been our friend until we have made it acidic and now fear its coming. The poor farmer who waits and prays for the rain that will loosen the soil and the roots also fears that it will pollute and ultimately sterilize the rich soil which is both his ancestor and his livelihood. Would that the rain, like the air, could be clean again, friendly again.

Personal experiences in significant moments of our lives often bring us to tears. Crying is both a release and a cleansing, a sign of intense caring, sadness at separation or joy at reunion. Tears are a work of compassion, a recognition of truth, a response to the reality that life presents. "I call forth tears, the aroma of the holy work."[17]

Music is a kind of water life, flowing through our veins, keeping us moist and moving, nourishing us, enabling us to cry, cleansing our systems, and helping our insides to stay in good working order. We borrow the music as we borrow the water and the air. These elements are impossible to own. When we think we have them "under control," they burst out of our containers and command our attention. They seem to have a life of their own, a movement and style that are not limited by our attempts to harness them.

If air and water are environmental indicators, of what is the quality of our music indicative? What does our art say about our environment, the space we make for ourselves? Is our aesthetic life polluted to the point of choking? Is our music gasping for air? Is music supported and cherished in our environment or taken for granted and used thoughtlessly, with no attention to the great wonder that is singing around us? Are we wasting our music as carelessly as we waste our water? Can the abuse of our music annoy us enough to wake us up to all kinds of pollution of our earth gifts? Can our thirst for clean and clear and friendly music draw us into a more active commitment to saving the water too?

"If there is magic on this planet, it is contained in water."[18]

Earth

You must teach your children that the ground beneath their feet is the ashes of our grandparents. So that they will respect the land, tell you children what we have taught our children, that the earth is our mother. Whatever befalls the earth befalls the children of the earth. If you spit upon the ground, you spit upon yourselves.

This we know, the earth does not belong to us; we belong to the earth. This we know. All things are connected like the blood which unites one family. All things are connected.[19]

—Chief Seattle, 1855

If there were to be an "Earth song," it might well be the last line of the text quoted above: "All things are connected." The four elements teach us that the energy of Earth is traded back and forth among its many creatures. Earth shares its richness—richness of texture, of color, of mineral deposits, of birthing possibilities, of growing power. Earth is a great dark womb, where the mysterious "dying" of seeds occurs, while we patiently wait outside. Earth grounds us. "Having one's feet on the ground" is an expression of good sense and wisdom, as opposed to "walking on air," when we may feel euphoric and a bit impractical. Being in touch with Earth's wisdom is connecting ourselves to our origins there and also to its mystery and its wealth of wisdom.

We have already considered Earth's connection to the virtue we call humility, a word which is related to the Latin root "humus" which means ground or earth. A true sense of humility in us means recognizing and celebrating our Earth-origins. It offers us, like primal people, an identification with our ancestry, and confidence that at life's end Earth will welcome and recycle our clay. Like water, air, and fire, Earth does not belong to us. Rather, we are people of Earth, with Earth features and processes. Wisdom and humility bring us to realize these connections and to work at doing our part in the fabric of creation.

The Hebrew story in Genesis Chapter 2 tells of our being made from the dust of Earth. Earth and air, water and a fiery spirit are all our ancestors. The humility of Earth people keeps us conscious of that ancestry. The multi-colored nature of Earth's soil is reflected in our own many-colored skins, its strength in our spinal resilience, its beauty in our handsome features, its healing in our own health and self-healing powers.

Our names for Earth do it little justice: dirt and soil have come to be unsightly; we speak of clothes being dirty and soiled. People who are dirty are considered disgusting and are shunned. Even people whose personalities might be described as "earthy" are an embarrassment to a society which holds cleanliness, sophistication, and polite conversation in high regard. People who acknowledge and celebrate their Earth connections are not always patient with such un-Earthy values. They can remind us that we must keep our feet on the ground.

If all things are connected, then we are connected to Earth in very origin-al ways. Our ecology is rooted in our awareness of this connection, rather than in some condescending, anthropocentric attitude which will work only for human survival (such as whisking a select human sampling away from the planet to build a new life). A growing movement toward recognition of planetary bio-regions focuses our connectedness with our precise living space, and hopes to treat Earth's dis-ease which has been brought on by our human lack of attention and arrogance. [20]

The Green Party movement, begun in West Germany but spreading rapidly, works at political recognition of this story of connections, and takes seriously the role of government as steward of Earth's vast resources. Its focus is the health of the planetary community, given the multifaceted global crisis in which we find ourselves. [21]

Another phase of the ecological movement is a return to Earth-practices like gardening, where interaction and co-operation with Earth help to restore humility as well as provide healthy food for our families. The selection and planting of seeds, the patient waiting for the sprouts, the cultivation, watering, and weeding, closely resemble the process of making art, and teach us to trust the mystery of the dark womb, growth, and fruit-bearing. Working with Earth as clay, the potter learns humility by being challenged by the clay's tendency to have a life of its own. Rather than being fashioned as the sculptor wishes, the stone may tend to reveal the shape that lies dormant in it. The best artist and the best gardener, like the best music-maker, work with the material, have power with it, rather than power over it. We find that trying to have power over the seeds, or the clay, or the cello results in frustration and tension.

That we are connected around the Earth is not accidental, since Earth's round shape insured that sooner or later its creatures would meet one another.

> A rounded Earth pressured human groups into intense and unavoidable interactions. The sphericity of the Earth demanded that the hominid types *deal* with one another. Precisely because of this demand our arts and science and religions and civilizations and cultures emerged. Quite simply put, the Earth's shape was *necessary* for human development... [22]

How we choose to face one another around the Earth is our choice. Do we take a cue from Earth's roundness and begin our circle-making. Or do we square off to see who is stronger, wealthier, wiser? And in what does our strength, wealth, and wisdom lie? Is it drawn from the center, from the mother, the Earth? Does our ownership (of land, water, minerals) result in stewardship? Do we recognize and celebrate that we are all connected?

Does music have its feet on the ground? Being grounded means acknowledging our connectedness to our Earth, listening to Earth-music, playing with it, dialoguing with it, having power with it. Some of Earth's vast richness is revealed in its music, played on its air, danced in its water, sung in its fire. Why should we have to be so afraid to get our hands dirty, when it is that dirt that has born our supple fingers for caressing the violin's bow? If all things are connected, and both primal people and contemporary science tell us that they are, then our music is connected to the Earth in a very element-ary way, and our music-making takes energy and life from Earth's great storehouse of creativity.

4

Earth Music

The basic dynamic of the creation-centered spiritual tradition is dialectical, as distinct from dualistic. Dualism creates a consciousness, and with it institutions and structures of either/or. One is either good or bad, male or female, strong or weak, spiritual or sensual, for example. Dialectical consciousness is about both/and thinking, both/and relationships. One can be good and bad, male and female, strong and weak, spiritual and sensual.[1]

We have looked at and wondered at the power of Earth's elements and have observed that their presence is significant for our music-making, both supporting and enhancing it. The elements are our partners in creating the music, and also our teachers. They reveal to us who we are, who they are, and who the Earth is. They help us to see that we cannot take a separate pride in being human, but that at all times we attribute the good and beauty of what we do to all our many ancestors and partners. This does not mean that we belittle the creative potential of the human species, but it does keep things in Earth-perspective. Next then, we should consider the "how" of the Earth. How does the Earth work? Is there a basic rhythm which is akin to our music-making rhythm? What can the Earth teach us about the "how" of music?

We will take our first cue from Matthew Fox's clarification about dualistic and dialectical thinking and acting. An example of the Earth's dialectical rhythm is light and darkness. Because of our unique relationship to the sun, our experience is both light and darkness. Both are important. We need the light of day for nourishment, for moving about

71

and growing, for seeing the wonders of creation, for expanding our horizons. We need the darkness of night for rest, for close-up vision, for story-telling and dreaming, for appreciating mystery. The Earth simply could not continue to exist without the day-to-night exchange of its light and darkness.

This dialectic is reflected in our human lives. Sometimes we feel "light"—eager to be about our work, connecting with others, growing, and feeling good about life. Other times we feel "dark," alone, confused, not able to see clearly. It is a wonder that these dark times are often periods of intense gestation. Something is happening in us, even though our vision of it, our understanding of it, may be difficult or blurred. This darkness is like the darkness of the ocean womb, or Earth's womb, or an animal womb. If we allow the Earth to teach us, we can learn not to be afraid of this darkness, but to trust it as we trust the Earth to help the seed to grow in its darkness. We may even learn to welcome the darkness as the environment and opportunity for gestation and birthing in our lives. It would be foolish to want to push back Earth's darkness, to expect that the sun will always shine on us. But often we expect our lives to be filled with the light of knowing, filled with an understanding that sees clearly. Mystics have tried to teach us that the darkness is very important in spirituality, that the times of our feeling alone or even abandoned are times for letting go, for paring down and fasting, for gaining perspective and divine wisdom. A poetic mystic of our own time reminds us of this.

You darkness, that I come from,
I love you more than all the fires
that fence in the world,
for the fire makes
a circle of light for everyone,
and then no one outside learns of you.

But the darkness pulls everything:
shapes and fires, animals and myself,
how easily it gathers them!—
power and people—

and it is possible a great energy
is moving near me.

I have faith in nights.[2]

Of course we are now able to control the immediate
darkness around us because of our discovery (not invention,
the Earth was doing it all along) of electricity. This Earth
power is a lately found gift (in terms of the history of the
universe) and it is welcome in our lives. But our ability to use
it may tempt us to forget the importance of the Earth-gift of
darkness. We may, in fact, push back the darkness around
our homes, just as we push back the darkness from our lives.
We may come to expect that we should always be in the light.
We are of the Earth and like the Earth. If our use of Earth
gifts divides us from it, makes us masters over it in such a
way that we pretend that we can live only in the light, we are
missing an important point: light is best understood and
cherished when it exists in partnership, in a dialectic, with
darkness.

> There is an appointed time for everything,
> and a time for every affair under the heavens.
> A time to be born, and a time to die;
> a time to plant, and a time to uproot the plant.
> A time to kill, and a time to heal;
> a time to tear down, and a time to build.
> A time to weep, and a time to laugh
> a time to mourn and a time to dance.
> A time to scatter stones, and a time to gather them,
> a time to embrace, and a time to be far from embraces.
> A time to seek, and a time to lose;
> a time to keep and a time to cast away.
> A time to rend, and a time to sew;
> a time to be silent, and a time to speak.
> A time to love, and a time to hate;
> a time of war, and a time of peace.[3]

Notice in this passage the repetition of the rather absolute
"There is ... " No question about it: Life is like this, darkness
and light, rending and sewing, dying and being born. The

Earth teaches us that there is a time for everything and its counterpart. We do not have to choose; life will present us with both.

A serious question arises here in relation to Christian theology which claims that we are "people of the light" and that darkness is gone forever because of the death and resurrection of Jesus Christ. Is it? Is that really how life is? Is that really what Jesus did—banish all darkness from our lives? Even in faith-filled lives, isn't there darkness, the darkness of death, of sorrow, of loss and confusion? The life of Jesus was filled with this kind of darkness, right to the very end. We tend to neglect his darkness just as we neglect our own because in fact we did not learn the greatest lesson of his death and resurrection. What Jesus showed us is that the darkness is not forever; the darkness of the cross and the tomb gives way to the bright light of rising. The darkness is partner with light in the dialectical movement which is our lives. We cannot rise without first dying; we cannot have fruit without letting go of the seed. Jesus teaches us that it is good to enter the darkness, and that the darkness is the place of promise, gestation, and rebirth. Rilke even tells us that the origin of this darkness is God.

> Yet no matter how deeply I go down into myself
> my God is dark, and like a webbing made
> of a hundred roots, that drink in silence. [4]

There are many ways in which the light/darkness dialectic is reflected in our music-making. Movements between major and minor tonalities provide variety. Often a major section is followed by a minor one for "contrast." The composer senses that either all major or all minor is simply not adequate for music-making, or may even be boring. Different moods and tempos may reflect light and darkness differently. Even key colors have variations: D Major is a brighter key than F Major. There are subtle differences even in the "light" of major sound, just as there are shadows and shades even in the brightest day.

Another light/darkness motif in music is sound and silence. One of the greatest music-makers of all time,

Wolfgang Amadeus Mozart, is supposed to have said, "I can tell a good musician by the way he plays the rests." This may seem like a surprising comment from a man who wrote a phenomenal amount of notes in his short lifetime. Yet it reveals something important about the dialectic in music: we must be attentive not only to the music which is sound, but also to the music which is not-sound. This is very obvious in a polyphonic piece: if all the voices are to be heard correctly, that is, as the composer intended, then rests in all voices must be strictly observed. When one voice is resting, another voice is heard, and the interweaving of sounds from different voices (and the interweaving of their silence) makes the music. If one voice were to become inattentive or arrogant and sing through the appointed rests, the other voices would not be heard and the music would suffer. This can be a parable for our lives. In life there is sound and silence, presence and absence. If we ignore the "rests" and cling to sound, or if we make some noise to fill up the silence, we never get a chance to relish the moments of nothingness between the notes, the suspension of sound, the breathing-in time.

> There's no music in a "rest," Katie, that I know of; but there's the making of music in it. And people are always missing that part of the life-melody; and scrambling on without counting—not that it's easy to count; but nothing on which so much depends ever is easy.[5]

A critical dualism in western thinking has been body/soul. The body is flesh, the soul is spirit; the body will die (return to dust), the soul will live forever (go to heaven or hell); the body is a prison, the soul is free. How can the Earth be corrective for us here? The Earth itself seems to be less clear than we are about the distinction between flesh and spirit, body and soul. We may think of Earth itself as inanimate material, an object. A closer look (especially with post-Einsteinian eyes) reveals intense goings-on, unaccountable changes and rhythms, growth and death side-by-side. Where do minerals come from? Why do rivers flow? What are the shifting continental plates doing? Why do seeds grow in soil?

Recall that the Genesis story of creation says "Let the earth bring forth..." Once Earth is created, it becomes a creator itself.[6] In embracing Earth-wisdom we look again at a subject that rational human thought has considered closed. The Earth is not just dirt; and as long as we continue to act as if it were, we are missing a great deal of its wealth and mystery, not to mention its teaching power. We have divided Earth from itself by acting as if we know better than the Earth. This dualism is reflected in our own division: body/soul, flesh/spirit, mind/heart. Our mechanistic model of the body has yielded rich data about how our systems work, but the machine doesn't tell us everything there is to know and understand about the human. The way we have addressed this problem in the past was to allow part of us to dominate; we chose the head. Thinking, logic, rational behavior, and "good sense" (functions of our left brain) have too long prevailed over intuition, feeling, imagining, dreaming, and experiential knowledge (functions of our right brain). In this choice we have shut ourselves out from half of living. Once again, science is helpful to us by opening up our understanding of the human brain, revealing to us its development and its incredible talents. Our work is to allow the right and left brains to function together, to help us to overcome the dualism of mind/heart, logic/intuition, verbal/non-verbal.[7]

These kinds of dualism have made us feel caught between the sides of a question; we are led to believe we must choose sides: good/bad, thinking/dreaming, male/female. Our resistance to choose may be a teaching time for us, a moment when we understand more clearly that the human is the species who can consciously create, who can open up questions, who can look at many options.

> If the world were merely seductive,
> that would be easy.
> If it were merely challenging,
> that would be no problem,
> but I arise in the morning
> torn between a desire to improve
> (or save) the world
> and a desire to enjoy (or savor)
> the world.
> This makes it hard to plan the day.[8]

If we look closely at the underlying rhythms of savor and save, we might see that they are really two sides of one very significant attitude. Because we savor something we work to save it, treasure it, keep it going, make sure there's more of it to pass on. Saving Earth without savoring it could reflect a condescending anthropocentric head trip that presumes that we humans know best what to do with/for Earth. In fact, this has been our attitude, and we are now realizing how woefully inadequate it has been. We have been self-serving, saving only ourselves and losing Earth and its resources. How much will we have to lose before we wake up to the inadequacy of the savior model of the human species?

The other extreme lets us off the hook entirely: sitting around savoring has its attractions, but only savoring is in fact not savoring at all. Our savoring of Earth should wake us up to what needs done about saving it, that is, keeping it safe and whole, so that it can continue to provide a healthy living space for future generations of creatures. We know that vacations are wonderful and necessary, but an eternal vacation would be boring. The human species has a serious task of stewardship, and our love for creation is what motivates us to keep busy at this work. The dialectic of work and rest is akin to that of savoring and saving. We work with the Earth to insure its good life, but as we work we are struck by Earth's own miraculous workings, and so we pause to wonder at it. In wondering we fall in love again and so have new energy for working. The work leads to rest, which leads us back to work again. The saving and savoring, the doing and not-doing, the left, the right, the body, the soul—all can and should have space and time in our lives.

Another contemporary dualism is that of male/female. Can our Earth music, its rhythm and light/dark melody be helpful in uncovering a deeper dialectic even in this most puzzling and intricate mystery? Many early myths recount the wedding of earth and sky, wind and water to begin "creation." The differentiation, two-ness, seems primal. And yet the newest story of the universe indicates a cosmic unity out of which, at some point, sexual differentiation evolved. Perhaps this differentiation was crucial to our coming to know what life was about. If we were all the same, what would be the purpose in dialogue? It is because we are different that we notice who we are in complement (or opposite) to others. If I am a white person who has never seen a person of color, my whiteness might not be significant to me. When I meet a very red or a very black person, I will notice my own whiteness. But then I may also reflect: How are we related if our colors are so different? What is underneath color? What is the human characteristic which is more primal than what color anybody is?

In relation to the male/female dualism we can then ask: Is there some-thing more primal, more original, than male/female? How am I most primally related to others?[9] Unmasking the dualism, revealing the dialectic of male/female will help us in our struggle to find words that will clearly and wonder-fully reveal what being human is about. The radical separation of traits which we have called "male" and "female" seems not to be helpful anymore. We want to find out what is healthy and human and authentic, what will challenge us to integrity and wholeness, what is the next step in the coming-to-fullness of the human species. We cannot deny that different cultures encourage some traits in women and others in men (for good or for ill). Whether or not these traits are essentially male or female, however, is open to question. What precedes, perhaps predates, male and female?[10] What words can we use to describe these human traits, including how varied and wondrous they are, that will help us out of dualism and into the dialectic?

An example of language not being helpful involves the popular comparison of Jacob's ladder and Sara's circle. Jacob's ladder refers to the vision recounted in Genesis 28:10-19, in which Jacob dreams of a ladder with its top reaching towards the heavens. The implication is that God is "up" and "over" us. Sara's circle comes to us from Genesis 18:9-15 and the consequent episode in Genesis 21:1-8. The significance of this story is that Sara can see humor in the situation of such an elderly couple giving birth and so she laughs. Her experience of God is very immediate; God is working very particularly in her life, and in a way that surprises her and causes her great delight. The circle is the image which indicates Sara's dancing laughter. In contemporary usage the ladder and the circle are tagged with the names of Jacob and Sara (although previously in this book the names have been eliminated). The question here is whether or not characterizing the ladder and the circle (and the experience of God which they connote) as male (Jacob) and female (Sara) is very helpful. The ladder image can be very evocative, revealing our tendency to categorize and package people, to want to "move up in the world," to climb, achieve, and succeed. The ladder shows us that our success is often acquired by stepping on or around other people. By contrast, the circle image shows that categories are not important, that people can move freely in and out in their lives, rather than up and down and that achievement is joy shared. Using these two images in relation to church and community life can be very helpful. Making the images male and female, however, gets in the way of the conversation as well as making some people defensive. The images are rich and powerful as they are. They help us into a more dialectical mode, a space where we can be free to explore the various implications of ladder and circle without taking sides.[11]

Our proposal in this chapter is that the music of Earth can teach us, and in teaching can also free us to move beyond differentiations which divide us (either personally, one from oneself, or communally, one from another) into clarifications and celebrations that will draw us together. Our bonding will not be accomplished by making us all the same—the music of Earth is as rich and varied as its many terrains and climates—but by allowing us to acknowledge our differences and then use them in our task as humans. Facing this task, the Earth music is our friend. It sings for us the primal wisdom of this planet; it leads us into its own planetary rhythm and multicolored melody; it embraces us in its all-welcoming harmony.

5

The Earth Takes Up the Words of Jesus

> With the development of human life, the standard had
> been growing, too. In Jesus' time one could expect more
> of a human community than in the time of the beginning
> of humanity.
>
> Even if someone would realize completely, and without
> fail, the older human standard of life, he would have
> fallen short of what became possible in the new order of
> human existence.[1]

If the initial and primal task of human species is to be in
touch with our universe-al origins, then we look for
guidance in this task to those who accompany us. We have
seen that the Earth itself is a primary teacher, both through
its elements and through its dialectical rhythm. But we also
can look to those of our own species who seem to be
particularly in touch with what it means to be human. And
so we look to the great religious figures. As one of those
figures, Jesus Christ has been held as a model of humility,
trust, reverence, creativity—all of the qualities we have
noted as important for music-making and global living.
Joseph Donders implies (in the quotation above) that Jesus
moved the human community forward in a significant way,
raising the standard of living, so to speak, asking more of the
human species. The sayings of Jesus remain for Christians
and also many non-Christians as truth for the human time
that has passed since he first spoke them. Even apart from
the context of their original parables, the wisdom of the
gospel stories is applicable to the many and complex conditions in which humans find themselves. Our question now

is, do these sayings have a "universe-al" significance? Can the Earth, the cosmos, take up the words of Jesus? Can the sayings of Jesus be expanded to reveal the wisdom of the universe? Can his words help us into a deeper hearing of the New Story as well as the most ancient wisdom of our planet?

One group of the sayings of Jesus literally relate to Earth wisdom and use Earth images.

> You are the salt of the earth; but if the salt has lost its taste, how shall its saltness be restored? It is no longer good for anything except to be thrown out and trodden under foot.
>
> Matthew 5:13

> Look at the birds of the air; they neither sow nor reap nor gather into barns, and yet (God) your heavenly Father (and Mother) feeds them. Are you not of more value than they? And which of you are by being anxious can add one cubit to your span of life? And why are you anxious about clothing? Consider the lilies of the field, how they grow; they neither toil nor spin; yet I tell you, even Solomon in all his glory was not arrayed like one of these.
>
> Matthew 6:26–29

> Truly, truly, I say to you, unless a grain of wheat falls into the earth and dies, it remains alone; but if it dies, it bears much fruit.
>
> John 12:24[2]

Let us pause to rehear these words now, as if they were being spoken by the Earth. What are the new dimensions which we experience as a result of this rehearing?

The Earth claims us as its own salt. In humility, grounded-ness, we recognize our connection to Earth, our origin there, but also our vocation to be its seasoning to help draw out the Earth's own flavor. The New Story of the cosmos teaches us that the purpose of the human species is to wonder at the Earth, to celebrate its beauty.

We are the self-reflection of the universe. We allow the universe to know and feel itself. So the universe is aware of itself through self-reflective mind, which unfurls in the human. We were brought forth so that these experiences of beauty could enter awareness.[3]

The Earth itself is unable to be conscious of and celebrate itself. It needs the human to do that. We are salt for this task. If we lose our flavor, our taste for this endeavor, or our courage, we are good for nothing as far as the universe is concerned. If we have not been awake to and in love with this planet and its universe, we miss the greatest opportunity ever presented to an Earthly species. We fall flat!

The Earth has brought forth its creatures and cares for them in its own "natural" way. This engendering presupposes on our part a radical kind of trust, but also a back-to-basics way of living which is one of the signs of global living. A simplicity in life style uncovers the fallacies of worrying about how to dress or where to live. It offers another more "origin-al" (organic) way of life, a simple style, not naive and passive, but one in touch with and respectfully imitative of the Earth's own style. And so the Earth could say, "Look at my birds and my flowers. They existed before there were human eyes to see them. But they longed to be seen and loved and so you humans were brought forth. How much more care have I lavished on you, so that you could see them and celebrate them. So don't separate yourself from me or from them; don't turn away and suppose that you can make it on your own. Trust the simplicity of my own life." (I am the vine, you are the branches, John 15:5)

The most dramatic of the literal uses of Earth images in the sayings of Jesus Christ is the "grain of wheat" passage from the Gospel of John. A truth of life is evoked from the story of the mysterious destiny of a seed: unless it dies it can't live and bear fruit. Amusing would be the idea of a seed that refuses to be pushed and broken open by the soil and the rain, stubbornly holding on to its identity, never guessing what it might yet become. Less amusing is our own unwillingness to be broken so that we can grow. No one looks forward to pain in life. Sometimes the being broken is forced upon us by life, whether we like it or not, as when we grieve at a friend's death. Even then we may hold on to the past, push the pain away, refuse to let it open us up to new life.

This experience of brokenness is the classic "via negativa," the way of darkness, of groping and confusion, the way of terror and beauty.[4] The Earth offers us an intimate, inside-the-womb glimpse at its own truth: things die in order to give new life. "Artificial" flowers pretend this is not so: "You don't have to die," they say. "You can stay the same, not change, and act as if the present will go on forever." The Earth challenges this statement with its own flowers, of incomparable beauty *and* brevity.

A second group of the sayings of Jesus which may have a new hearing now as words of our Earth are the challenging statements where the false wisdom of the self-proclaimed "wise" is unmasked.

> Who are my mother and my brothers?... Whoever does the will of God is my brother, and sister, and mother.
>
> Mark 3:32,35

> Am I not allowed to do what I choose with what belongs to me? Or do you begrudge my generosity? So the last will be first, and the first be last.
>
> Matthew 20:15-16

> Take these things away; you shall not make God's house a house of trade.
>
> John 2:16

Once again, we allow space to rehear these sayings as if the Earth were speaking them.

The question "Who is my mother, my brother, my sister?" may sound harsh to us, considering that Mark tells us that Jesus' own mother was standing outside. When we ask it now we are not casting off our particular human family. In fact what we are doing is opening up many channels of relationship to a much broader community. Things are not

84

as determined or as limited as they seem, even in our own parentage. Lots of creatures have passed their lives to us, many more now share the ups and downs with us.

Stand at the ocean and ask: Who is my mother?
Bless the meat on the plate and ask: Who is my brother?
Look at the lilies of the field and wonder:
 Who are my sisters?

Once again Earth helps us to open up our thinking and feeling about who our parents are, who the creatures are who have given and continue to give us life.

The third saying quoted above offers two "morals" to the parable that precedes it. The first moral is "don't be upset because I will be generous." Earth is rich and fertile in many places and dry and barren in others, unpredictable and violent in others. The Earth does not owe us a pleasant living. We owe the Earth our energy for good, simple, cooperative living. It is not wise, nor particularly helpful, to get angry at the Earth because it is dry or wet or split open. Its forces as well as its gentle gifts are beyond our control. Ultimately the Earth will be who it is.

The political arrangements occasioned by our greed for the Earth's gifts are often unjust. We trample the poor so that we can be well-fed and warm. We displace native people so that we can take the Earth's space and resources.[5] We tear down rain forests essential for the Earth's balance so that we can grow more beef.[6] We are ravenous for food and fuel, for precious minerals and land. We take rather than share, and make enemies rather than friends. How can we as global community on a round planet continue to think that our jealousy and enmity will sooner or later not take its toll on all of us?

The second moral which closes the parable in Matthew 20 is "the last will be the first, and the first last." What better image for this moral than the circle.

For it is precisely in a circle that the first are last; the last are first; and, what is more to the point, no one knows who is first, who is last, and above all, no one cares.[7]

Finally the Earth can well claim that it has been meant to be a house of prayer for all peoples, a welcome place, a sacred trust, room for creatures to be free. But we humans have made it a "house of trade," a den of thieves where people steal and are stolen, abuse and are victim, kill and are killed. Will Earth also cleanse itself of this decay? Who will announce the day and banish the first of the Earth abusers and thieves?

A third group of sayings whose meaning is enlarged in our own time are the words of lament.

> What an unbelieving and perverse lot you are! How long must I remain with you? How long can I endure you?
>
> Luke 9:41[8]

> O Jerusalem, Jerusalem, killing the prophets and stoning those who are sent to you! How often would I have gathered your children together as a hen gathers her brood under her wings, and you would not! Behold, your house is forsaken.
>
> Luke 13:34–35a

How long will the Earth endure her destructive children? Will all of your plundering go unaccounted for, unanswered?

> The earth will not be reduced to abject servitude. After all man's assaults the majesty of the earth stands over against him with an inscrutable countenance. There are gathering signs of a response in the form of massive retaliation. The game is a game but only if it leads to larger life. Else the game is no longer a creative experience but a struggle to the death which man cannot win.[9]

As Rachel wept for her children, as Jesus wept for Jerusalem, does not Earth now lament her betrayal by her children, that special species waited and longed for by generations of unseen and unseeing years? Will the Earth's compassion extend to us who are blind and deaf to her laments?

Finally, three poignant sayings of Jesus are heard as he faces death.

86

Take, eat; this is my body; ... Drink of it, all of you; for
this is my blood of the covenant, which is poured out
for many for the forgiveness of sins.

Matthew 26:26–28

My soul is very sorrowful, even to death; remain here,
and watch with me.

Matthew 26:38

My God, my God, why have you forsaken me?

Matthew 27:46

There is no question that the Earth has given and
continues to give its own body and blood for our "salvation"
as its creatures. Its bodily energy and richness are given into
seeds and roots to make food. Its life energy and water are
wetness and growing power for us. Perhaps one of our
mistakes about the Earth's body has been like our mistake
about the Body of Christ, the eucharist. We

watch eucharist, rather than do it;
think that eucharist will make everything easy and take
   pain away;
focus on the Body of Christ as bread to the exclusion
   of the Body of Christ as us.

These are serious indictments for Christians who consider
themselves eucharistic people. We have watched the priest
say the Mass, make the eucharist. Our response was to
receive "It." It is time that we begin to do eucharist—make it
together, as concelebrants, share it as a sign of our willingness to be eucharist, to allow our own bodies to be broken
and our blood poured out. This is the primal challenge of
liturgical renewal in the Christian churches.

Having received eucharist, we presume that its effect will
be calm and peace, problems solved, hurts healed. Rather,
eucharist is food for the strength to face the problems and
the pain. It is model for working at life, not tranquilizer for
escaping. It is bread for moving out to others, not for
keeping private. In Paul's first letter to the Corinthians, he
scolds the Christian community for not being attentive to
one another.

When you meet together, it is not the Sovereign's supper that you eat. For in eating, each one goes ahead with their own meal, and one is hungry and another is drunk. What! Do you not have houses to eat and drink in? Or do you despise the church of God and humiliate those who have nothing? [10]

1 Corinthians 11:20-22

Paul says very clearly: You cannot be attentive to the Body of Christ as you celebrate it in the Lord's Supper and not be attentive to the Body of Christ as you see it in each other. This challenge rings through the centuries to our own time, when churches wage battles over recipes for eucharistic bread while people go hungry at the door or in the very pews of the church.

Does this challenge also address our treatment of the body of the Earth? We certainly have treated the Earth as an object, an "it" rather than as our living ancestor and home. We have come to believe that Earth and its science will provide answers to the problems we create out of ignorance and carelessness. Won't the Earth clean up after us, de-pollute its rivers, resolve the problem of nuclear waste? We have used and used up Earth's resources for more than enough food, and been inattentive to the reality that the Earth is us and we are the Earth. That inattention to the planet is harmful and inconsistent with our intended stewardship of it. We are not just creatures on the Earth; we are of it and with it. We are the Earth's body and blood. What do we do in memory of her?

The twenty-sixth chapter of Matthew recalls the scene in the garden of Gethsemane where we hear the words of Jesus as he confronts his own death. He longs for the support of his friends and asks them to keep vigil with him even though they are unable to understand the great struggle in which he is involved, a struggle that was about to take his life. What happens when we transpose his words to be an Earth-song? The plea is real: "Remain here, watch, pray." The Earth needs its creatures to be compassionate, to watch with it, as the disciples were invited to watch with Jesus. He wanted them to feel his passion, not his physical suffering, as much

88

as the intensity of his love and his energy for life. And what happened? The disciples fell asleep. We also have fallen asleep to the mystery of Earth, to its passion for life, its intense love and labor for our birthing. Like the disciples, we must wake up (even be reprimanded) before the hour of our delivery is at hand.

Does Earth feel abandoned by its Creator? What will be the answer to its final plea: Why have you forsaken me? What answer did Jesus receive? The first was silence, nothing. How can we interpret the silence of God after this primal scream from the cross? Isn't it a scandal that God did not intervene?

God is the gardener, Jesus is the seed. The seed is planted, the gardener waits, knowing the seed must die. When the seed cries out for rescue, what can the gardener answer? The planter could remove the seed from the ground, but what good would that be? That would be—literally—fruitless. The seed has to learn to let go, of everything, and then be incredibly surprised by what it will become. The gardener's answer is silence (I can't rescue you.), then surprise (You're a tomato!).

The Creator's first response to the Son is also silence: "I can't rescue you; that's not the kind of God I am. I'm not waiting out there to fix things for you. I am with you and in you even in this despair and darkness; that's just the kind of God I will be." We might imagine Jesus saying, "You're right, I don't want to be like that either...into your hands I commend my spirit...I want to be like you...I let go, I am broken."

The Creator's second answer is surprise...resurrection ...new creation...life. Not "fixed," not rescued, not unpassionate, but passionate, transformed, recreated—the risen Jesus explodes from the tomb.

The Earth is waiting, hoping not to be forsaken, but trusting its own darkness. There are those who claim that God will fix it for us. But the crucifixion scene confounds us, unmasks our false hope: no "deus ex machina," no mechanical Mr. Fix-it-God. The earth is waiting. God is waiting. Will both be forsaken?

89

PART III

Playing Music from the Rocks

Introduction

Challenged by the amazing revelations of the new cosmological story and the recovery of a primal world view (all things are connected), human beings now review their origins to see if what they know about their beginnings affects how they live their lives. New worlds of heritage and ancestry appear on the vast horizon of human memory. The species has been asking "Where did we come from?" as long as it has been a self-conscious species.

The answer to this question is far from clear, and some of us are still afraid of the question. When we now ask, "Where does the music come from?" our intention is less to answer the question than to keep it open before us. In fact, there is no absolute and for-certain, historically provable answer to the question of music's origin, except the broad one of "somewhere, somehow, in the universe." The importance of raising the question lies in its power to open our ears to hear music in new places and to realize and acknowledge that the music-making activity is not simply a human venture. Earth has brought forth this special gift from its own resources, the very rocks into which it cooled following its separation and differentiation as a planet. All that we now know came from that rock. Some of the music may still lie struck in this magic rock, waiting for ears more sensitive and more disciplined than we now have. Will future music-makers start listening to rocks again?

The painter goes walking to stretch her eyes, to clear her vision, to try out a new way of seeing which may result in a very new way of painting. We will go walking now through some of music's space, to stretch our ears and their hearing, to open up our thinking about music so that we can explore new sounds. We are not dealing here with a history of music (as in Palestrina to Schoenberg) but with the experimental story: How does a person come by music? Where does it rise in us? How do we hear and respond to it? What will help us hear better? What is music's value for the human species?

6

Music in Personal Evolution and Development

My work in music education has been concentrated mostly in three fields:

1) Try to discover whatever creative potential children may have for making music of their own;

2) To introduce students of all ages to the sounds of the environment; to treat the world soundspace as a musical composition of which man is the principal composer; and to make critical judgments that would lead to its improvement;

3) To discover a nexus or gathering-place where all the arts may meet and develop together harmoniously.

To this I would add a fourth field which I am just beginning to explore: the uses to which oriental philosophies can be put in the training of artists and musicians of the West.[1]

It is probable that for most of us the first experience of music is a listening one. We may even hear music while still in our mother's womb.[2] In those early moments musical sound may not even be differentiated, but heard as a part of the vast, mysterious, somewhat frightening, external "world." In the early musical education of children, developing the skill of listening is very important: listen to the beat, listen to high and low, fast and slow, sad and happy. The ear is the operative organ here, not only as a rational instrument, but as access into the whole body. The ear is not the only way to know music, however, as attested by hearing impaired people who feel music in a way that hearing people cannot.[3]

Children tend to respond to music with their whole bodies. Although this kind of musical experience is fun and creative, there is a broader implication for the child's development. Our contemporary scientific data reveals that our human brain has three "levels": the outermost brain is the Neomammalian portion, the "human" brain, the rational and creative part of us. This is the residence of the right and left brain areas. Inside, underneath this, is the Paleomammalian brain, inherited from non-human ancestors; this part of our brain is responsible for emotional behavior. Finally, inside those is the reptilian brain (oldest of all), the part responsible for our body movement and coordination. The best learning situation is one in which all three levels of the brain are involved: the rational and creative, the emotional, and the movement abilities. There are certain activities of childhood that help develop these brain areas. For example, crawling is an important part of the child's motor development. People who did not crawl as children often later experience coordination problems. Having children respond to music through the creative movement of their bodies engages all three areas of the brain. Dance response draws on the reptilian talents of body movement as well as the interpretive, emotional mammalian skills. Furthermore, it also draws on the initiative and non-verbal articulation of what is heard and engages the outer brain, the specifically human talent. Full body interpretation of the music, then, not only enhances our "appreciation" of the music (at an intellectual level) but strengthens our connecting power, our full-brain activity, and so our total well-rounded development as a human person.

Another aspect of the music listening activity is its teaching power. We begin learning music because listening to it engages us and we want to be a part of it. A child begins to talk by repeating words and phrases that it hears. These words and phrases become tools when the young person begins putting them together creatively to express meaning. He or she learns that the arrangement of words has significance, sends a message, communicates a need or a new insight. Listening to music invokes a similar process: hearing and repeating enable the listener to develop skills for becoming a music-maker. As children repeat (echo) their first strains of music, they should be encouraged to play with the music, to test it out, to use the basic musical sounds to make their own music. This can involve the use of an instrument, but the voice should not be excluded. Various methods of music education encourage "free singing" responses to sung questions from the teacher, where no musical answer is "wrong." This technique reflects a philosophy that people have music in them, rather than an attitude that music must be taught to them.

This playing with musical sound, whether with voice or instrument, also involves testing out sounds, seeing what sounds make more musical sense to the player or singer, what sounds might be surprising and fresh. This kind of experimentation is like that of the composer who sits at the piano and improvises to "get the juices going." The composer may then sketch out ideas and play with them, testing various answers to musical questions that evolve, or trying different harmonies or rhythms. This kind of free improvisation gives the creative impulse room to develop its own unique talents.

To return to the analogy of learning to speak, a child develops patterns that sound good, that draw upon the wealth of material accumulated in listening. Testing often involves making mistakes and receiving advice from friendly adults. Children who are encouraged to experiment with musical sounds will also draw upon things they have heard. The richer the listening experience, the broader the material from which to draw.

One particular method of music education is based on the "primal" song and movement of children, using a common game song melody and the basic pace of walking and running. This developmental approach to music became the official music curriculum in Hungary. Zolton Kodály, the developer of this system, used folk material as well as newly composed songs, children's games, and nursery tunes. "He wished to see an educational system that could produce a people to whom music was not a way to make a living but a way of life."[4] In Kodály's method the educator begins with music that comes "naturally" to children, particularly the melodic third, the pattern

sol   sol   mi   la   sol   mi

(As in "John-ny has a girl-friend.")

and walking and running movements. Kodály's use of hand signals to accompany the singing of pitches of the major scale, a system first developed by John Curwen in 1870, invites the "whole brain" to work while the music is happening. Carl Orff, working in Austria, also used many of the same ideas, but strongly incorporated the use of instruments. Both of these music education programs involve children in the creative use of the music that is already in them, and the teaching of skills as a naming of the experience of the music. Children feel the movement of running and walking and then begin to name it. They match and echo the melodic patterns in conjunction with large body movement and then the more refined hand signals, and finally learn how to write them. In both cases children are encouraged to use the skills they learn to begin creating their own rhythms and melodies.

Playing and testing teach us two important values which will be helpful in many areas of life. The first is the ability to imagine. Making music requires letting go of old ideas and opening up to new ones. Imagination helps us blur the lines between pretty and ugly or right and wrong. It requires giving yourself space and time to explore lots of possibilities. This development of imagination is important for music-making, but also for other areas of our lives. Time and space to play with ideas and options encourage and nourish our creativity.

What do the toys our children play with teach them? Do the toys do everything themselves or do they engage the child's imagination to make them work? Let's suppose the worst: a child plays only with push-button, self-propelled, automatic, unbreakable toys (including TV). The imagination is rarely called into play, creative thinking is not needed, all answers are supplied (not necessarily the best answers). As a child grows, she or he must make choices for life. How does one decide to become a doctor or a musician or an horticulturalist? One way is to imagine what it will feel like to spend your day looking down people's throats, or practicing for hours, or worrying about the lilies freezing in the greenhouse. Testing and trying out, imagining what one might want to be, will be helpful in making a good decision. What if the skill of imagining has been unattended and undeveloped? Where will the child turn?—To answers that others will give, or to apathy, thinking that one decision is as good as another. The self-actualizing potential will lie dormant; a decision may be made (or fallen into), but the real power to choose has not been exercised.[5]

The second value that playing with music teaches is one of pruning. The composer who plays with the music (adult professional or child with the xylophone) will have to make choices, decide on a tune, rhythm, patterns, and form. Otherwise the music cannot be written down and shared. This decision involves self-pruning a willingness to let go of some ideas, although they may be good ones, in which case they can be saved for another time and another tune. The choice must be made if the music is to be heard.[6] Likewise, one's life involves some self-pruning, an ability to make choices and to let go of things once a choice has been made. Some people spend their lives worrying about what could have been. Precious time and energy are lost, not to mention personal development. If many options have been explored and weighed, a person will have less of a feeling that he or she missed something.

Although a child needs time to freely explore music and sound, tools and skills are needed to allow for broader or more complex expressions. As children refine motor skills, they are able to play rhythms that are more intricate and demand precision. From larger body movements we move to smaller, more complex steps, which explore the beauty of more developed abilities. Skills for writing down this more complex music enable children to share their music with others, as well as to have it performed again and again. As more skills are needed for notating what is heard, more are taught, just as skills in grammar and writing are taught when the need for these arises in the child's life.

What we are working at here is a style of music education that draws music out of children, inviting then into its experience and creation, rather than playing it at them, or teaching then skills that do not seem relevant to them. As we have noted, listening and imitating are important, but only as one aspect of musical (and human) development. Children at their best are not unaccustomed to finding magic in rocks. Who knows what music they may find there?

Our discussion of music education presumed that music can help us to develop some skills which are important for our living. Another way to test this theory is to look at the music-making process to see if it can be a model for other areas of our lives. We have already noted how well the attitudes for quality music-making address our global living problems. Let us now see if the process (the underlying movement and dynamic) and techniques used in making music will be helpful for our personal lives. For the sake of clarity we will use a specific example, that of a choir director choosing new music for the choir.

The first movement of the process is the introduction of the new piece.[7] Perhaps the choir director hears it at a concert, or on a record, or even unearths the piece on the music shelf of the local library or music store. The listening or reading experience evokes a response—buy the music or forget it. Suppose the musician is intrigued enough to buy one copy to take home. The second movement then begins: the get-acquainted time. The musician plays through the various parts and the accompaniment to get a feel for the music. Some pieces reveal themselves readily, others are more opaque. This part of the process requires patient and careful study, perhaps more reading and research about the particular style or period of composition. There may be a lot of puzzling and confusion, darkness and mystery, a need for some gestation time until the music comes clear. Then one of two things can happen.

1. The director decides the piece is not worth the work of rehearsal. Sometimes compositions that look good on paper are disappointing when heard. (The reverse, however, can also be true: music that looks too simple or even trite on paper may turn out to be worthwhile when well-performed.) Or the director may realize that the piece is too challenging or inappropriate for this choir at this time. The director may even give up on learning the piece herself, not being willing to put work and study into the venture. In all of these cases there is a "breakdown": the relationship between the musician and the piece of music is over, or at least put on hold.

2. The musician is captivated by the music, reverences it, works at it long enough to uncover its mystery. Patience is exercised in this learning; sometimes one even gets angry and goes away for a bit. This may be precisely the time when one is approaching "breakthrough"—the "Aha" moment— "So that's how it goes!" In this case, the order is placed, the music purchased, and the piece given new life through the director's affirmation of its beauty.

When the music is presented to the choir, the director has a new role: introducing and teaching the music to the singers. Most likely they will go through the same learning process as already described, although it may be facilitated by the director's first-learning and already enthusiastic acceptance of the music. The singers may need as much or more time and patience before reaching a breakthrough, particularly if they are new singers or have difficulty reading music. It occasionally happens that a director is unsuccessful in communicating enthusiasm for the music, and no matter what ploy is tried, the choir is headed for breakdown: "Where did you find this?" and "Can we send it back?"

Meantime, what is the choir director doing? Being a co-creator. The music has already been created and written down by the composer, who now relies on others to bring the music to life. So the director takes up this task, teaching, encouraging, leading and shaping, always with a vision for what the piece can or should be. The vision is shaped by the director's own particular talent, style, and musical training. The strength and clarity of this vision, as well as the ability of the director to analyze problems and try different techniques, is what will often get a choir through a difficult piece. Co-creating is hard work, often distressing, sometimes nearly overwhelming. Choir directors who have experienced the moments of breakthrough with a singing group will testify, however, to the excitement and sense of accomplishment and pleasure released when that moment happens. The breakthrough then enables the singers to become co-creators as well. This choir's performance of a piece will sound different than any other. By their attention to and respect for its nature they will give it new life, allow it to be heard again, perhaps even by another choir director.

Throughout this learning time, both director and choir begin to own the piece of music, not in the sense of exclusivity, but in the sense of recognition and familiarity. This kind of ownership enables the director to be even more demanding and precise in the interpretation and performance of the piece. The struggling and care contribute to the depth of the ownership and so to the strength of the eventual performance.

Now suppose at this point in the process the director collected the music and put it away. The choir, if they have had an authentic breakthrough, would cry out in dismay and disappointment. The whole idea is that the music is worked at so that it can be shared, performed, heard by others. Not to do so would betray all the energy, time, and hard work which had gone into the piece. We could, of course, wait for the piece to be perfect. But most choir directors will know when a piece is "ready"—which may not mean perfect.

To retrace the process in brief form:

We—hear the music, begin a relationship with it;
  —work at it, to understand and learn it,
      sometimes with great difficulty,
    but hopefully come to a point of
    "breakthrough" when we
  —are able to be co-creators with the composer, and
  —share the music in performance.

The question originally posed was whether or not the process of music-making had something to tell us about life, that is, can we learn from this process skills and insights for better living? One way to answer this question is to look at other creative ventures to see if they follow a similar pattern. Let us take gardening as an example.

The initial excitement about gardening (the beginning of the relationship) involves buying seed, laying out the garden, preparing the soil, and generally being enough engaged by the vision of the harvest to put work into the project. When the seeds are planted, there is little to do except wait and be patient until they begin sprouting. There may be dismay at empty spaces where seeds fail to sprout or take extra long to do so. There is mystery and gestation happening in the dark womb of the earth. The gardener encourages the sun, waters the earth, and waits. When the sprouts appear the gardener becomes more active, cultivating, weeding, feeding, sheltering, and staking. The gardener is co-creator with the plants, the soil, the sun, and the rain. There would certainly be something very wrong about then leaving the fruits of the vine on the vine to die. The whole idea of the garden is to share the fruit of the labor. To do otherwise simply doesn't make sense. This gardening process follows the same basic movements as those of music-making: initial engagement, hard work and patience with the mystery, co-creation, and sharing the fruits. The reader is free to reflect on other life-works, like cooking, raising children, writing poetry, and so on, to see if this process also applies to such activities. We will proceed, however, to the life-project itself to see if the movements of the music-making process (and the gardening process) can teach us about life.

We are the image of God. Our initial engagement is with divinity, when God's breath is gasped for the first time. Our task is to reverence and cherish our life, to celebrate and bless it. This will involve lots of mystery, patience, and hard work. Some of us are tempted to give up, some do so. But others who are enticed by life's richness experience many, many breakthroughs, when life makes sense—both in its light and its darkness, its grief and its joy, its blessing and its pain. When we experience life's breakthroughs we are empowered to become co-creators of our own lives, to have power with, to make significant choices, to exercise our own

101

energy and talent for shaping ourselves. As we do so, we become capable of friendship and love, of sharing our insights and enthusiasm with others, of bearing pain with them, of being compassionate in the sense of moving with them through whatever life brings. We can even come to trust the ultimate breakthrough which life offers us: Death!

How does the musician know when it's time to perform the music? How does the gardener know when the potatoes are ready to be dug? As co-creators, musicians and gardeners learn trust—of the music, of the earth, of the seeds, but most of all, of themselves. With experience the musician knows when the music is ready, and the gardener knows when the potatoes are ripe even though they are hidden in the hills of earth. The temptation is to hesitate, wait for some sign, be overly cautious. But then you may miss the ripest moment.

The experience needed is practice of the process, trusting that the potatoes will be there because the gardening activity has produced potatoes before. With experience we know that the darkness and the mystery will yield to creation and fruit, whether potatoes or music. Sometimes there's a moment of release, of letting go: I've done everything I can do, now I must trust myself to know that this is the time—to harvest, to play the music, to let my child go. Learning to trust oneself and one's own judgment is an important part of the music-making process. Perhaps it is trust in themselves, born in long hours of music-making, that makes musicians (and other artists) so suspect to institutions that rely on people's lack of trust in themselves to give meaning and purpose to the institution. When people do not trust their own experience and their own thoughts, they will look to the institution for guidance and answers. When an institution wants to survive, it needs people to need it—it relies on their dependence to keep itself going. There is no one to tell the painter when the painting is done; there is no one to tell the composer when the symphony is finished. The artist must simply "know." Artists learn to trust their own instincts about their work, its development and its integrity. How could it be different then with the rest of their living? This truth is illustrated in Irving Stone's novel about Michelangelo, *The Agony and the Ecstasy*. The scene is the Sistine Chapel where Michelangelo has been working on the ceiling painting for more than four years. This dialogue between the Pope and Michelangelo occurs:

> "When will it be finished?"
> "When I have satisfied myself."
> "Satisfied yourself in what? You have already taken four full years."
> "In the matter of art, Holy Father."
> "It is my pleasure that you finish it in a matter of days."
> "It will be done, Holy Father, when it is done."[8]

If the artistic process, the music-making process, can be a model for us in our personal lives, then the element of trust emerges as a key skill for individual development. We have suggested that people can learn skills for personal growth by sharing the music-making process. But often art (music) is the place where people really fail to trust themselves.

> The single largest obstacle in teaching adults to meditate by means of art is getting them to let go of judgemental attitudes toward their self-expression. The judgemental attitudes have been passed down to most members of our society from the youngest age: "You can't sing," or "You don't dance well," or, "You can't draw at all." [9]

It would be difficult to estimate how many people have lost interest in or inclination toward music-making because others have told them they are not musical. There is no need to deny that some people are more musical than others. We need them to pursue music as their life's work, and we should support them, emotionally as well as financially. But this doesn't mean that music is all taken care of and doesn't need the rest of us or can't find a space in our lives. Part of the listening and learning experiences of childhood should be the use of one's own body (voice, feet, fingers) to make music. This experience is as important to personal development as learning to throw a ball or a plant a seed. There are a variety of ways to express and participate in life. Music is one that is available to all of us.

Often you hear church professionals say that people won't sing in church unless they have something to sing about. So we can ask, what is the first thing a person sings about? If the implication of the church question is that people should sing about faith, then we can ask, what is the first thing a person has faith (trust) in?[10] It seems that the answer to both questions should be—your own life and life experience. Before an articulation of religion, a child should experience the dynamic of life (both in light and darkness)—that it is good to be alive, that what life offers you can be rich, challenging, creative, and transforming.

Birth is a blessing, and singing is a way of blessing life. This blessing is both pain and pleasure, sadness and joy, because life is full of the dialectical dynamic. It offers both our pleasure and our pain for blessing. Singing, in its darkness and light, major and minor, sound and silence, can reflect the dialectic of life for us. That is the first thing anyone can sing about. But those who come to be church should be especially alive to sing about their faith (trust) in life. Whatever the life experience at the present moment, the song helps us to greet life, to welcome all that it brings, to continue to recognize ourselves as valuable creatures, creatures to be trusted, especially by ourselves. The professional musician among us has the difficult and awesome task of helping others into their own songs, of teaching the songs that have helped the community down through the ages, of offering new songs that recognize and celebrate the new stories. In doing so, the musician must unmask the sins of mistrust that prevent us from exercising our creativity, and enable us to uncover the magic and mystery of the life process.

7

Music in Time

Women, in becoming who we are, are living in a
qualitative, organic time that escapes the measurements
of the system. For example, women who sit in institu-
tional committee meetings without surrendering to the
purposes and goals set forth by the male-dominated
structure, are literally working on our own time while
perhaps appearing to be working "on company time."
The center of our activities is organic, in such a way that
events are more significant than clocks. This boundary
living is a way of being in and out of "the system." It
entails a refusal of false clarity. Essentially it is being
alive now, which in its deepest dimension is participation
in the unfolding of God. [1]

We have closely examined the process of music-making in
personal experience and discovered that it parallels other life
processes. Like life, music-making exists in time and also
uses time. And yet the time of music-making is not simply
linear, although a given opus will take a certain number of
minutes, depending on the tempo established by the conductor. The questions about time that are apropos to this
discussion, however, are: What is the quality of music's
time? What kind of time is music in? How does music affect
time? Is music time-less? And most importantly: Can
music's relationship to time teach us about our life-time?
Before directly addressing these questions we should
reflect on two kinds of time, as illuminated by Mary Daly in
the quotation which opens this chapter. One type of time is
linear, historical, and able to be recorded, measured, and
allotted. In this kind of time the past is definitely over and the
future stretches out in numbered years toward infinity. As

105

each day passes, it is logged into the vast record of time past. The image that emerges here is one of passing through a gate called present, being checked in, the past behind us, receding, the future mapped out ahead. This kind of image eliminates any opportunity for experience of mystery in the present moment or for human ability to influence or work with time. Time as we name it only exists AS we name it. Minutes and hours exist because we have named them and put them on our clocks. Now clocks control all our human activities. There are many limitations to living time in this way, by the clock, but one of the most obvious is that it is boring. Work is this kind of time for many people. They slowly count the passage of hours until quitting time, or days until Friday. This time feels dry and lifeless, boxed in, not capable of any excitement. The usage of days is accounted for before the week starts, with no chance for a side excursion or a surprise. This time is humorless and unfeeling, and it takes its toll on us while offering few rewards. In this time "waiting" is the essence of bondage. Because the object of time in this scenario is to get somewhere other than where one is, waiting is painful and frustrating. But waiting is also eternal, because the present moment is impotent. We wait for the weekend (unless you're a church organist), wait for Christmas, wait for retirement, wait for heaven. Something better is always down the road but never here right now.

The good news is that there is more to life than this. There is another kind of time which humans have the power to name. It is time that recognizes and respects the rich possibilities of the present moment. Refusing to believe that time should be so lifeless and boring, we can also refuse to be in bondage to it. This second kind of time is imaged by a spiral where the past and future are circling and swirling around the present. There is energy, movement, and excitement in the spiral. The past is not gone. Rather, its energy is gathered up into the dynamic of human memory which enables all things past to be present to us. The future is not so far away but in fact is here already waiting to be evoked. With this experience of time, work that might otherwise be drudgery becomes alive with possibilities.

More is happening than what meets the eye if all levels of our brain are awake to life. In this kind of time waiting becomes an opportunity to look around, to notice and appreciate what otherwise might be missed, to see the humor in the quirks of the human adventure, and to call others to notice also. Waiting is time for understanding and acknowledging the value of that for which we are waiting. While awaiting the arrival of a friend one already enjoys her presence, relishing who she is and anticipating the good time to be shared. Waiting or preparing for a vacation or a party is sometimes as much fun as the event itself. This kind of time is not strictly chronological, but more open ended and more "spacey" in the sense of full of possibilities. It offers new and surprising answers to the question: What time is it? It's time to plant, time to reap. It's time to make love, or time to refrain from love-making.

Although music exists in time and takes time to perform, it is also beyond time. Where is the symphony when it is not being played? What time do we feel passing while singing a Bach cantata? What is the quality of music-making time?

Chronologically, a piece of music may be old, having been composed centuries ago. But in this moment of music-making, it is reborn, given life again (which life it couldn't have if we weren't playing/singing/listening). The past is spiraling into this present moment. Tomorrow's rendition of the same piece is already present in this moment, and yet that performance is guaranteed to be different than today's.

How can music's challenge of the tyranny of chronological clock time be helpful in the human experience of time? Music opens up time for us, offers a new sense of the quality of time, brings past and future into present, blurs distinctions between them, and raises questions about past or future always being better than the present. Human lives may be recorded chronologically, but human beings must resist submitting to only this sense of time. Confusion about how we are "in" and "with" time may result in in-human decision making.

An example of this confusion occurred recently on a radio talk show when the host asked a woman caller how she felt about the possibility of her son being drafted for the army.

Her response was, "Before I was a mother, I was an American." This woman chose to go only by chronological time, in this case, calendar time. According to her own naming of her experience, earlier in her life-time she was an American, but later "became" a mother after literally giving birth. The question, however, is not one of chronology of the past, but essence of the present: Who are you now, primarily? What aspect of you is more you than other aspects? Are you at this moment of choice a mother (from the inside out) or more an American (from the outside in)? Another way to say this would be that if this woman had been born in another country, she could still be a woman. The nationality is accidental to her life, whereas the woman-hood is more essential. Before there were nations and national wars there were women. Hopefully as we move into global civilization, women and men will recognize that national distinctions are not essential and therefore not something we should go to war about. Our ethnic back-grounds enrich our lives, but do not keep us separate. But the woman in this radio interview will find global living very difficult because her national standing will keep her from seeing the tremendous opportunity for circling and dancing together. This woman's conviction is indicative of far too many "Americans" who support programs, politics, and war-making efforts that are in-human. The absurdity of her sense of her own time, her life-time, reveals how cleverly our ownership of time has been distorted and how crucial it is to unmask the fallacy that chronological time is all that matters.

We can look to other activities in addition to music for a new sense of time "out of time." Our valuing these timeless moments enables us to be free to "waste" time—making music, making good conversation, sitting at the ocean, sharing in a ritual. Ritual time, like music time, invites us out of linear time into a timelessness that frees us from the demands of the clock and encourages us to be in touch with our own reality in time. Ritual is a place where "mother-hood" and "being an American" should come into focus and dialogue with one another. Ritual should allow for and promote past, present, and future evoking one another, so that past does not necessarily take precedence, nor are future's promises longed for so intensely that present's opportunities are missed.

We could ask, "When does the ritual begin?" Chronologically we answer: "Two o'clock." Another answer might be: "When the people are all there." The gathering of the people is the essential thing for the ritual to begin. In fact, the gathering of the people is, in a way, already the ritual so that one could answer: "When the people begin to gather" or "When they set about gathering" or "When they get up, when they dress the children," or even "When they make the decision to come." The party seldom begins at the clock time written on the invitation, and yet the day of the party has a special feeling, a sense of anticipation, of waiting and readiness that already is party. The timing of ritual is not clock time, nor should it be hampered by clock time (we have to clear the parking lot for the next group). The time should be determined by the ritual, not vice-versa. Since artists are skilled at timing (When is the painting done? When is the anthem ready?), their presence at planning for ritual is crucial. Their willingness to be free of clock time can also help us to be free; the musician's sense of sound and silence, darkness and light, of what kind of singing is good for what "time" it is, should be nourished and recognized rather than feared or mistrusted.

Since time past and time present are always with us, how we feel about them is important. There are two ways in which people can relate to the past as well as be able to sense what is prior in the reality of the present moment. The first is through memory—remembering in a way that allows things to be what they are. A second way is through sentimentality—remembering in a way that tends to manipulate, to make things as we would have liked them to be. Here is a comparison of these two ways of thinking.

Memory	Sentimentality
	As I look at the past
I own what I remember	What I remember owns (obsesses) me
I can critique the past	The past is glossed over

109

The past is very revealing, showing life as it really was	The past is unclear, afraid to see life as it really was
I can give pain meaning	I can't deal with pain
I can dialogue with the past	I complain and gripe, perhaps am angry

Then in the present

I have power to act	I am powerless, feel listless
I can move forward	I want to go back to the "the good old days"
I am subject	I am object
I can focus on the moment	I am distracted by the past
I realize things change and will die (e.g., real flowers)	I pretend that things don't change and will continue forever (e.g., artificial flowers)
Things are what they seem	Things act like something else
I can make an investment (e.g., write a letter)	I will resist investment (e.g., buy a greeting card)

The most promising revelation of this comparison is that a healthy memory is enabling in the present moment. Because we are honest with ourselves we recognize that the past was not all light, but that there was darkness there as well. This should help us to see that the same is true of the present. When we invoke memory we enable the past to stand before us and teach us, and as a result we are empowered for acting in the present, for choosing freely. If there was pain and difficulty in the past we can forgive it, but remember it in a way that we still learn its lesson. With a healthy memory we have power with the past and power with the present.

Unfreedom seems to be the clearest revelation of the list of things under sentimentality. In this way of remembering, the past is able to have power over us and keep us in its bondage. We are unwilling to forgive past pain and so it eats at us, although we probably don't recognize this. At the same time we settle for expressions of sentimentality that do not accurately reflect life. We gloss over the past and we gloss over the present, and we are never really satisfied with anything. Consequently we complain and gripe, and often come across as angry people, although the object of our anger is unclear. Perhaps the object is unmet expectations, both for the past and the present. But rather than looking honestly at the anger, dialoguing with it, and learning from it, we wallow in it and remain unable to act, to choose something different or better in the present moment.

Music-making is possible because of our human memory—because we can gather up the skills and lessons of the past and allow them to work for us in the present. Musicians must have healthy memories and a good sense of the potential of the present moment even to begin to make music. If musicians would be sentimental people they might only admire the work of past masters, but be afraid to play their music, worrying that this present rendition would never be enough. This kind of attitude stops the music-making process and the music.

We have already seen that having power with the music is essential. This means looking at the past honestly and critically, celebrating the music of many ages past, but eager to hear the music that is being written in our own time. A musical group needs a balanced repertoire—the proven pieces that tradition hands down to us, as well as the unproven but challenging and exciting music that can be accompaniment for the New Story of the cosmos. Music and music-making encourage us to move out of chronological time and into the flowing and spiraling time of the music of the ages. Ancient music can be heard and played again now. Present music is tried out and evaluated, perhaps reminding us of older times, perhaps challenging our ears and our imaginations to hear a music that is newer than time. Music plays with and on time, and encourages us to do the same, celebrating past and present, and eagerly looking for the music that will shape future time, that will open us and keep us circling and dancing.

> At the still point of the turning world. Neither flesh
>   nor fleshless;
> Neither from nor towards; at the still point, there the
>   dance is,

111

But neither arrest nor movement. And do not call it
   fixity,
Where past and future are gathered. Neither movement
   from nor towards,
Neither ascent nor decline. Except for the point, the
   still point,
There would be no dance, and there is only the dance.[2]

If a healthy memory is an important tool for relating to the past and the present, what guides us into the unfolding future, the future which is already present within us? As we have noted, future too often is always future; we are always waiting for something else, someone else, something more or better (like heaven), always putting off pleasure or rest until a better time. There is wisdom in saving money for vacationing or saving time for celebration, but only if the vacation or the celebration will be realities. Allowing the drudgery approach to work to control one's life while working toward a retirement that won't be enjoyed, because one's good health was unattended while working, is a cruel irony. The present cannot be frittered away into some eternal but senseless future, a future that may, in fact, never come. Like the past and present, the future must already be in us and in our choosing and dialoguing. If we look for a future that is unconnected to the present, we may never find our way there. If we are not looking at the future at all, or still wandering around in the past, the future will happen "to" us (have power over us) rather than "in" and "with" us (we have power with time, with the future).

Christian religions have not always been helpful in this task of balancing present and future. In fact they have often preached that "this life" is not really important, except as it prepares us for "eternal life." Storing up for eternal life, working at "being happy in heaven," makes it acceptable to live unhappily now. In fact, yearning for the passing of this life becomes a virtue. We are always relating to some ambiguous future, while missing the richness and the pain of the present. This philosophy (theology?) encourages us to ignore oppression, not to become responsible for correcting injustices, to keep our faith separate from "secular concerns" because "religion has to do with eternal life not this one."

The creation-centered spiritual tradition experiences sacred time very differently. It rejects the dualism of heaven/earth, and works and prays, as Jesus did, that the divine "kingdom/queendom of God come on earth as it is in heaven." While not denying unrealized eschatology, while not covering its eyes to the poignancy of injustice and sin and sadness in this life, its response is not to flee the present for either a more heavenly future or a more miraculous past. Rather, its response is to trust (i.e., believe) so deeply in the depths of the present that realized eschatology becomes reality. Realized eschatology is the experience that Now is the time; Now is the place; Now is the occasion; Now is the bringing together of the best of the past and the future; Now is the moment of divine breakthrough . . . [3]

This approach helps the believer into the tension and opportunity of present-future time. We look toward a future of fullness of life and justice, but in the meantime don't wait for someone else to make it happen, even God. If God didn't "fix things" for Jesus Christ, why should we expect God to "fix things" for us? Claiming the divine origin and sustenance of all life does not isolate us from life's problems or pains, or relieve us from responsibility for working at those problems and facing those pains. Rather, we take up the time we live in, with whatever it offers us. And on that time we play the music that will make us a new creation, that will enable us to act and choose and give our energy toward the coming of the future. The time of the present is not opportunity to be missed. Every second, every beat of the music is possibility, revelation, consciousness of life. Music does not belittle time. Why should religion? Music values and respects time and teaches us to do so. Should religion do any less?

8

Choreography and the Cosmic Christ

Since Jesus was born and grew to full stature, and died,
everything has continued to move forward *because Christ
is not yet fully formed*: he has not yet gathered about him the
last folds of his robe of flesh and of love which is made up
of his faithful followers. The mystical Christ has not yet
attained to his full growth; and therefore the same is
true of the cosmic Christ. Both of these are simultane-
ously in the state of being and becoming... [1]

Our path in this section has been to use music as a parable
for personal experience and for the use and value of time. In
all of this it has been very obvious that music is not, cannot
be, an "it," an object. Music is an activity, a verb. Music represents activities of life for us: its rhythm, melody, and
harmony teach us about the rhythm, melody, and harmony
of life. Its process reflects the dynamic of our lives. Its
respect for time opens up our own thinking about time's
passage. At this point we turn outward and ask: How does
music address the rest of creation? Can music reflect the
evolving universe?

When one studies the New Story of the cosmos and the
place of the human species in it, one word jumps to mind—
"dance." Cosmic dancing is a good phrase to describe the
movements of planets and stars. There is relationship and
mutual respect. The stars and planets are attentive to their
own space, their own uniqueness, and yet they always move
in relationship to one another. The music of the spheres
sounds through a spacious universe, activating rocks, lunar
landscapes, and planetary rings. The choreography of the
planets amazes our small human onlooking eyes, and we
wonder what keeps it all going, what primal force causes

them not to stray but move steadily outward and apart from one another, still in the bursting out path of the initial fireball.

And what is the human choreographic task? Where does the human species fit into star-dancing? For Native Americans, the most important thing to do with your life is to be connected to the universe, to be in touch and related and listening. The Great Spirit is present and revealed in the tiniest creatures as well as the open prairie skies. Relationship to God is not separate from other human activities because all activity happens in relation to the universe. This cannot be denied or escaped, and for Native Americans, never forgotten. A significant aspect of Native ritual is dance. Sun dances, rain dances, dances to enact visions are all an integral part of life. These dances are not only imitative of the cosmic dance (the stars, the atoms) but a participation in it. This participation theme is what links primal understandings of the universe with contemporary scientific data. Humans do share in the cosmic dance of the universe. In the dancing the music is the prime subject. Music's rhythm enables us to join in dancing, just as the rhythm of the universe holds the planets and stars in time. Melody, adding color and mood, enhances our rhythmic gestures; harmony fills out the spaces and widens our dancing to include many strands of music.

Who are the ones who can lead this cosmic dancing? Who will teach us the steps? Who will call the circle together and begin? Chardin would probably answer: the cosmic Christ. The elements of many a dance are colorfully present in his description of the coming fullness of evolution with the Christ leading the way: the folds of the flowing garment, the loving followers, the creative and joyful activity of moving out and becoming. Christianity proclaims that this Christ is the Word made flesh. But this Word is not a static or only verbal one. The creative speaking of God results in all kinds of activity. Things are put in motion when the Creator speaks.

> Every time God opened his mouth in those first stories
> of creation, part of the world of life came into existence
> or was changed. God said: air; and winds began to howl

116

with pleasure. God said: earth; and that earth has not stopped settling since. God said: animals; and the birds began to whistle, the fish never stopped swimming, and all kinds of animals started to mate, reproducing the joy of their lives.[2]

The activity of Jesus in history was not creative of a new universe, but his spoken word was always an invitation to new life and freedom. This is why the Apostle Paul writes that in Christ we are a new creation.[3] Christians recognize that Jesus is the clearest image of the Creator, the one who shows us how to be human, the one who most evidences the task of the human species. The words of Jesus are filled with energy and life, challenge and compassion. The Aramaic word for "rejoice" is the same as the word for "dance," so that when Jesus told people to rejoice he was in fact telling them to get into the dance of life.[4] The dance of those who were healed was a dance of freedom and responsibility: Go and sin no more...Go show yourselves to the priest...Go and tell what you've seen and heard, what God has done for you. The cosmic dancing of stars and planets had gone on for millions of years, but someone was needed to choreograph human participation in this dance. The time was ready and full—the cosmic Christ appeared.

> Jesus did not come just like that. He came at the moment when the earth and the world were ready for him. He came when humanity had reached a certain degree of maturity in its evolution. He came at the point when it would have been impossible to go on without him.[5]

We uncover here a sense of anticipation, a readiness for something or someone to happen. The waiting of the world was full—the time was ripe, and the Creator, the origin-al Imaginer, knew that moment. We call it Incarnation.

It is possible that this kind of thinking helps us to answer the question "When did music come to us? When did it begin, and who were the first musicians?" We can see cave paintings from pre-historic times that show people making music with instruments, but it is impossible to say exactly when the idea of making music occurred to anyone. What seems likely is that music happened (was heard or was dreamed of) when the time for it was ripe, when the ears were sharp enough to hear it, voices strong enough to sing it, and fingers flexible enough to make it. What a tremendous explosion of creativity must have followed such a discovery. Centuries later we are still exploring its richness.

Opponents of a creation-centered theology often claim that such theology is all fun and pleasure and not serious enough for the problems of the day. In this scenario, where everyone is dancing, how does one address "sin"? Thus far we have used a musical metaphor for exploring life. It is possible that we can test it even further? In other words, are the sins against music-making helpful in uncovering the sins in a world still asleep to its cosmic connections? For this test we return again to our music-making process in which we:

—hear the music, begin a relationship with it;
—work at it, to understand and learn it, sometimes
    with great difficulty and in the darkness of
    puzzlement and confusion;
    but hopefully coming to a point of
    breakthrough when we then
—are able to be co-creators with the composer and
—share the music in performance.

Retracing the movements of the process, we note where things could break down, what would stop the flow of energy and enthusiasm. What would sabotage the music-making? What would be detrimental or even harmful to the musicians?

In the first movement, music is experienced (heard or read through) and a relationship between the music and the musician has begun. In these early moments the relationship is characterized by excitement at the vision the new music presents. The learner blesses the music and the composer, and his or her own musicianship is enhanced. The piece is pronounced valuable and the musician celebrates this fortunate discovery. Possible breakdowns in this initial enthusiasm could be caused by

—arrogance on the part of the musician who is not open
    to the mystery of new music; this may be related to

118

—apathy, an unwillingness to care enough, to be
engaged by the music, to fall in love again;

—lack of trust in oneself which prevents the
musician from taking the risk (Suppose I fail?
Suppose I'm not good enough to perform the piece?);

—fear of an experience of newness and where that
might lead.

Although no one would say that these breakdowns are
morally "wrong," they do represent a preoccupation with
keeping oneself intact, an inability to move out and greet the
world, an unwillingness to be caught up by something other
than self. One might wonder whether a musician who
practices these patterns of "sin" ever goes dancing.

The second movement of the process is a very likely place
for a music-making process to fall apart. The musician must
be willing to let go of preconceived ideas and allow the new
music (and its composer) to lead on. Sometimes musicians
are biased against certain styles or periods and are unable to
let go enough to hear something good there. At other times
they may be afraid of the hard work, even upset, that
working with new music will cause in their lives. In this part
of the process there is darkness and mystery, frustration,
even anger at the music's unwillingness to be easily understood or played. Dying to old ideas and patterns can be very
difficult; entering the mystery of a new piece of music just
might change you. "Sin" in this movement would be
refusing to let go and be led by the music, clogging up the
learning process with self-doubt and mistrust. The musician
may well give up here and avoid the birth pains involved in
coming to know and perform a new piece.

In the third part of the process the musician takes the risk
of being co-creative. From the darkness and mystery a vision
begins to emerge, and the excitement of becoming a new
creation gives fresh zeal to the process. The music gives new
life to the performer by sharing its secret beauties and inner
mysteries. Often the performance will involve new and
original interpretations because something new has happened between the music (the composer) and this musician.

Refusing to co-create is a deadly sin for any artist. Stopping up the life energy whose movement is toward creating something new betrays the gift of being an artist. Being unwilling to co-create means not allowing the music to flow, not allowing different kinds of music to be born, not trusting oneself enough to believe that you can be a co-creator.

Finally, not to share the music—as we have already seen—is an unforgivable wrongness. What pleasure is gained from only private renditions, no matter how exciting and how innovative? To refuse to play or sing for others is to hold back life. It disrupts the cosmic dancing and quiets the music's universe-al call.

We must now ask whether these breakdowns in the music-making process, these "sins" against music's life, are comparable to the problems and sins of the rest of our lives. Arrogance is a significant wrongness in a world working at cosmic connecting. We have already noted that human arrogance has not only distorted history and the human understanding of our origins and our task, but also threatens the life systems of the planet. We are still unwilling to see that polluting the air and the water with the waste of human industry and consumption is ultimately self-polluting and self-destruction. Our eyes look too far over the heads of non-human creatures to notice that they share life with us. We become concerned only when our thoughtless waste begins to cost us our health and comfort. Even then we are reluctant because corrective measures will disrupt the economy. Surely arrogance is a sinful attitude which prevents us from developing our most human talents and from taking the steps necessary to ensure our planet's future. Arrogant people have difficulty in the circling dance of the cosmos, since they are impatient with creatures less agile than themselves.

Apathy, not wanting to be bothered, not allowing oneself to be swept off one's feet, to be engaged or to care, is a self-protective sin which is still as rampant as arrogance even though both should be outmoded by this time. We should know better by now than to think that we can sit on the sidelines of the universe. If we allowed ourselves to let go and become involved, our compassion would draw us into working to save what is still saveable. Apathy relies on a God who will fix things, or it may be underlined by a pessimism about the human project: nothing I do will matter anyway.

A lack of trust in oneself often goes under the guise of a false humility (I'm not good enough or I can't be creative). Oppressive institutions need people who do not trust themselves so that the fallacies of the institution can continue. If I can't trust my own sense about what clothing is appropriate for me, I have to believe what designers and manufacturers tell me I should wear.[6] If I can't trust my own sense about what is right and wrong, I have to wait for a church to tell me. If I can't trust my own leanings toward what to do with my life, I put it on God and say, "I feel called..." What's wrong with saying "I want to be a minister, a missionary, a social activist"? When we are afraid to take the risk and the initiative, we say "God is calling me to..." If we don't trust ourselves with our own lives, how can we possibly be co-creators? If we don't trust ourselves, how can we trust one another? In this sinful state of mistrust the whole community breaks down, suspicion and doubt reign, and cosmic dancing becomes an absurd notion of a suspect few. Doesn't this sound vaguely familiar?

Finally, we have often held back fear of the new and what it might mean for us or cost us. We are secure about what is known and reluctant to try something new, especially if that might mean admitting we've been asleep. If we see life as a process of waking up (which can happen many, many times), then we will realize that past limitations and mistakes are not "wrong," so that we need feel guilt and regret. Rather they are times when we are asleep, not seeing or hearing or feeling what was going on around us. Waking up can be a shattering experience, turning one's world upside down. But being paralyzed by guilt or regret because of one's past is not helpful. Learning from it, dialoguing with it, and remembering it will be instructive and growth-producing. The fear of feeling guilt keeps many people from trying something new or different.[7] The fear of failing, of being embarrassed or scolded (I told you so) can be paralyzing. If musicians don't overcome this fear, music will never be heard in the land. If all of us don't wake up to the impotence our fears are engendering in us, life will not be heard or seen on the planet.

121

Letting go of old ideas and securities and moving into unknown territory is risky business. Moving into the darkness and pain of life, allowing oneself to be exposed and vulnerable is frightening, although with practice one learns that the darkness is opportunity for cleansing, challenge to break open and grow, place of gestation and nourishment. If we live life openly, life will lead us into its own darkness. The loss of a job because of conflict in values or style can be a painful darkness. Personal losses in death are sharp and encompassing. In both instances there is much to let go of and much to be discerned. Despite people's hesitancy to face the darkness life brings, they often miss the opportunity to learn from it because they cling to the hurt and pain, grieving over all kinds of deaths for years and years. Wounds that are unattended will not only not heal but will become infected and spread to other body parts.

When we hold on to the pain of our wounds, refusing to attend to them, work through them, acknowledge their depth and mystery, we are not only losing their powerful teaching potential, we enable their temptation to mistrust and fear to infect the rest of our lives, leaving pockets of darkness into which we are afraid to reach. We become angry and bitter and layered over with distrust and cynicism. When we finally seek healing because our lives are broken and meaningless, it may take months and years of peeling off layers to arrive at the place or places where the unattended wound still festers. It takes skill and compassion on the part of the healer to stand by as these wounds are opened and finally treated, while the wounded person often experiences anger and guilt at having the past resurface and exposed to the fresh air. With a new experience of trust and being trusted, even people who have practiced holding on to pain for most of their lives can be freed up to learn to face the darkness, even welcome it as opportunity and blessing.

Once people are willing to enter the darkness as opportunity, they are freed to become creative, to trust themselves to give birth to new ideas and images. The sin here is to refuse to bear fruits of the learning time, to keep for oneself the visions experienced in the darkness. Not to allow oneself to be born or to give birth is denying being made in

the image of God who is the original Creator. This sin
becomes one of blasphemy: I can't be creative, I can't imagine
God, I can't (God can't) do that.

Why is it that some people
do not bear fruit?
It is because they are so busy clinging
to their egotistical attachments
and so afraid of letting go and letting be
that they have no trust
either in God
or in themselves.
Love cannot distrust.
It can only await the good trustfully.
No person
could ever trust God too much.
Nothing people ever do
is as appropriate
as great trust in God.
with such trust,
God never fails to accomplish great things.[8]

The sin of "I can't" is rampant in cultures in which creativity
is laid on artists and the rest of the population is excused.[9]
Creativity is painful, messy, unpredictable, upsetting to
schedule-makers and ladder-climbers. But it is the moment
of *breakthrough* of the divine, a revelation, a birthing of God.

Finally, not sharing what has been realized in us—what
we have learned, not speaking out of the truth we have come
to know, not working to wake up others, to free them from
the injustice and oppression of fear and mistrust—is a
wrongness. True pleasure (blessing) wants to be shared,
wants others to come to this goodness also. The excitement
of new insights, new images, new convictions and visions
must not be contained or detained. Refusing to allow our
personal transformations to engage others is to disrupt the
momentum of the cosmic dancing. The energy of this life
process gathers and builds to overflowing into activity for
others. There is no holding back for those who have learned
to trust themselves and their visions.

If these are the sins against the movement of cosmic life

within us, then what virtues should we be extolling and teaching our children? Celebrating connectedness, true (earthy) humility, care and compassion, trust, risk-taking, embracing darkness, readiness to grow and change, mystical experiences, vision-seeking, being willing to be creative (image God), sharing oneself, waking up to others, letting God explode into creation circling and dancing and singing. Even more "traditional" values, like sacrifice and asceticism, may find new meaning and life in relation to our life process. The root meaning of sacrifice is to "make holy," not to "give up," as we often think. How do we make our lives and our time holy? Not by giving it up as much as by reverencing and celebrating it. Ironically, those who celebrate life most radically and freely are often the ones whose lives are taken, since we are not accustomed to such dancing in our midst. Asceticism can be a value in preparation for life experiences. Fasting is a cleansing in readiness for vision-seeking. It can also be a sign of solidarity with those who do not have the luxury of fasting, who fast because they have no food. Or it can be an action taken as witness to one's willingness to take only what one needs for living, not to store up or hoard. Our problem in the past has been to replace living with asceticism, to take on extra darknesses while avoiding the real darkness which life presents to us. "Holiness" does not mean withdrawal or escape from life, but running into life, which includes meeting and welcoming the darkness.

What better lead could we have in this project of life than Jesus Christ, whose connectedness to others, whose compassion, trust, and risk-taking comprise the stories on the pages of the Christian New Testament. Jesus ran into life and embraced its richness, including its darkness and mystery. He did not shrink back as Scripture says, but embraced the darkness of death.[10] And then, in fulfillment of his life process, Jesus was transformed into ultimate sharing of his life, becoming the "first born" of many sons and daughters.

One of the best Christian images for helping us to experience the cosmic Christ is that of the Body of Christ, sometimes called the "Mystical Body of Christ." Early in this book we looked at the human body as an image of integration. The human body functions as a whole and should be treated as such. We noted the mistake often made in using medical treatment based on a Newtonian parts mentality where only body "parts" were treated without consideration of the whole body, or where foreign substances are injected and cause side effects or other unexpected problems. Wholistic philosophies tell us that the body has tremendous self-healing powers, and that medical treatment ought to be engaged in order to help the body heal itself. We will now expand this image even further, by raising these same questions about the cosmic, mystical body of Christ.

A primary question for the functioning of the human body is one of appropriate amounts and kinds of food. The goal is a balanced diet, supplying what the body needs, but not so much that the systems get clogged up. Now we ask: On what does the Body of Christ feed? Is the Body sufficiently nourished by its word and eucharist? Do Christians receive a diet balanced in blessing and trust, or is it weakened by regular feeding on guilt and private sinfulness, by diluted presentations of word and contradictory signs in eucharist? When people are overfed, their systems get clogged up; or they may feel satisfied, thinking that they don't need anything else. They fall asleep. The smug character of many Christian prayers reveals an overconfidence in this abundant feeding, having all hungers filled. The lack of any creative, transforming activities in some churches seems to indicate that these satisfied people have fallen asleep. Are Christians over-fed on junk food rituals, but really starving for the food of passionate living and justice-making? Who in the Body will announce an end to this Bodily abuse?

When the Body is out of sorts and needs healing, where does it look? We have said that the human body is at its best as self-healer, and that medical treatment should assist the body in healing itself, by working with the body systems to keep them functioning. Let us try this out on the Body of Christ. The sacraments of healing still represent to too many people an injection of grace, a quick cure. The rituals have presented external substances (like absolution) to take care of the wounds. Healthy parts of the Body have understood the absolutions as help in the self-healing

125

process. But less healthy members have looked for a "fix," something to make it all better again, while the real problems (wounds) go unattended. As blindly as some people take what the doctor prescribes without asking what it is, how it works, or whether there are side effects, other people take the sacramental doses which churches dole out for their "souls." The Body of Christ must begin to work at healing itself also, allowing the members to exercise responsibility for functioning of the Body.

A companion question is: How do we exercise the Body of Christ? A smooth running human body needs regular exercise to keep it in shape. What is the exercise that will insure the good health of the Body of Christ? When are its strengths tested and stretched and its flabby muscles called to task? (Maybe the churches should begin cosmic dance classes.) One of the marvels of the human body is that, when one is practiced in listening, the body knows and reveals what it needs. We may be out of practice at listening but we can get back into practicing again. This does not mean hypochondria, for the body will demand less attention in the long run if it is cared for regularly. We are talking about an appropriate, compassionate attention to our body and its health. Can we trust the Body of Christ in the same way? Can we expect that it will also know what is best for it and say it? Will we respond soon enough to get back in tune? Or is our inattention terminal?

> For the body does not consist of one member but many. If the foot should say, "Because I am not a hand, I do not belong to the body," that would not make it any less a part of the body. And if the ear should say, "Because I am not an eye, I do not belong to the body," that would not make it any less a part of the body. If the whole body were an eye, where would be the hearing? If the whole body were an ear, where would be the sense of smell? But, as it is, God arranged the organs in the body, each one of them, as God'chose. If all were a single organ, where would be the body? As it is, there are many parts, yet one body...If one member suffers, all suffer together; if one member is honored, all rejoice together.[11]

One of the sins against cosmic living that we have named is anthropocentrism, that is, being concerned only about what people see and feel, what people need and want, to the exclusion of the rest of creation. The extinction of hundreds of species of creatures on a regular basis, and the wasting of precious earth resources are a direct result of thinking that human welfare is the only topic on our planetary agenda. A comparable religious sin has been attention to the welfare of the soul while down-playing, even despising, the body. While this sin has been given a little attention, church people still don't trust the body and resist its celebration at ritual (for example, liturgical dance). The good health of the human body requires that no part of the body can think that it is more important than the other. Paul uses the human body image and draws an analogy for the Body of Christ; we extend his analogy to the cosmic Body of Christ. One planet should not say to another: I don't need you. All planets are part of the universe, along with stars, comets, and various other heavenly creatures. Rather, a planet celebrates its relationship to all the members of its galaxy and the universe. As human creatures on the planet we cannot say to other creatures, "We don't need you. You are not important to this body." What do the members of the Body of Christ say to one another? How do they feel about the role of the various members? If the human body is hurting, our attention goes to that part of the body that feels pain. Is this also what happens in the Body of Christ? Does our attention (prayer, concern, money) go to those members who are hurting?

The cosmic Body of Christ reaches all those whom Christians call saints. The communion of saints is the gathering of all those who have gone before us as well as all of us. Anthropocentrism has limited our vision of this communion since we have only admitted people. The cosmic story opens up this Body to include all kinds of creatures who have been our ancestors, who have had trust (faith) in life and themselves. The psalms of Hebrew Scriptures are helpful here, especially Psalms 8, 19, 29, 47, 65, 93, 96, 98, 104, 136, and 148. These psalms remind us that it is the privilege as well as the responsibility of all creation, of all the members of the cosmic body, to sing and dance in praise. From the initial choreography of the planets and stars to the now refined steps of human interactions, we are led by the one in whom the dancing and the circling originates.

> I cannot dance, O Lord,
> unless you lead me.
> If you will
> that I leap joyfully
> then you must be the first to dance
> and to sing!
>
> Then, and only then,
> will I leap for love.
>
> Then will I soar
> from love to knowledge,
> from knowledge to fruition,
> from fruition to beyond
> all human sense.
> And there
> I will remain
> and circle for evermore. [12]

Finally, in case Chardin and Mechtild and the music itself are not enough to get us into the dance, then we have the example of the cosmic Christ himself in this Christian hymn.

I Danced in the Morning

1.	I	danced	in	the				
2.	I	danced	for	the				
3.	I	danced	on	the				
4.	I	danced	on	a				
5.	They	cut	me					

morn-ing	when the	world	was be - gun,	And I	danced	in the
scribe	and the	phar - i - see,	But	they	would-n't
Sab - bath	and I	cured	the	lame:	The	ho - ly	peo - ple
Fri - day	when the	sky	turned	black;	It's	hard	to
down	and I	leap	up	high;		I	am	the

moon   and   the   stars   and   the   sun,   And   I
dance,   and   they   would-n't fol - low   me;   I
said   it   was   a   shame.   They
dance   with   the   dev - il   on   your back.   They
life   that - 'll   nev - er, nev - er   die;   I'll

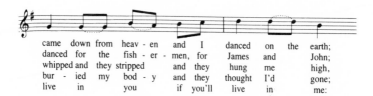

came down from heav - en   and   I   danced on   the   earth;
danced for the   fish - er - men, for   James   and   John;
whipped and they stripped and   they   hung   me   high,
bur - ied my   bod - y   and   they   thought I'd   gone;
live   in   you   if   you'll live   in   me:

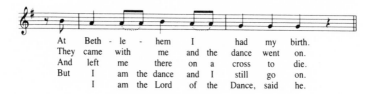

At   Beth - le - hem   I   had   my   birth.
They came   with   me   and the dance went on.
And   left   me   there on   a   cross to   die.
But   I   am the dance and I   still go   on.
      I   am the Lord   of the Dance, said he.

Dance then wher - ev - er you may be;   I   am the Lord of the

Dance, said he, And I'll   lead you   all,   wher - ev - er you may be,

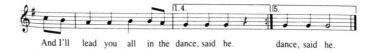

And I'll lead you   all   in the dance, said he.   dance, said he.

9

Music As Ritual

What if there were new music in churches and a variety of music? What if hopeful music were sung in times of tragedy and tragic music were sung in times of hope? What if jazz masses really caught on? What if ministers strolled the aisles? What if sanctuaries were abandoned? What if some churches were institutions dedicated to keeping people off balance, rather than enclaves of security? What if some churches were institutions directed toward shaking people's confidence in past dogma, rather than academies for indoctrination? What if some church were one place where one could expect novel acts and ideas, rather than one place for frightened, insecure people? What if the greatest danger in going to some churches was not falling asleep but getting overwrought?[1]

Our dialogue between the human image and the cosmic Body of Christ has yielded some important insights. Ongoing care for the Body of Christ is the focus of Christian rituals (like sacraments). Our final exploration about music, its origins, and its richness deals directly with ritual. Often we hear about music "in" ritual; now it is time to talk about music "as" ritual.

The energy for making music comes to us through thousands of ancestors. We trace its origins back to the original burst of the fireball, when all the energy that now activates us was released in that explosion of creativity. The question of music's energy, then, just like the question of human energy, is a connecting one. We are reminded that all creatures, even the tiniest, the least visible, the hardly audible, are connected by the origin-al energy of creation.

We get energy for music-making by drawing on and calling out the energy still stored in us, in the earth (through plants who feed on the sun), in the air, in the rocks. Music plays with the energy that has been waiting for millions of years to be evoked by human voice and hands, to be activated by the one creature who can hear and celebrate what music is.

This kind of work is magic work.[2] We don't understand where music comes from or where it goes; but while it is sounding in our midst it is a mysterious messenger from eons of cosmic life. Its rhythm, melody, and harmony captivate us, lift and caress us, toss us about, break through the complacency of even the most determined silence. Music is a lasting invitation into the creative magic of the universe. In this sense music is a sacrament of the cosmos. Its grace value is less salvational than co-creational. The music doesn't pretend to save us, but it does entice us into co-creation, even if we are only listeners. It connects us with others and with the dance of the universe. It invites us to hear and celebrate in a way that no other creature can. Because of that it evokes what is most especially human about us.

It is a mistake to think that music's power is simply soothing and relaxing. Some music pretends to be so, like that played on your local "easy listening" FM radio station. This kind of sound has a drugging effect, a mindless lulling of whatever might really be lurking in life. When we explored harmony in music we realized that not all harmony sounds pleasant, some harmony is dissonant. This is because music reflects all of life, light as well as darkness, joy as well as grief, understanding as well as confusion, beauty as well as terror. The earth is a violent as well as a beautiful place; earthquakes, tornadoes, and volcanoes remind us of that. There is terror in the seed being broken, at least from the seed's point of view. There is terror and pain in the slaughter of animals, whose insides are "cleaned up" and made hardly recognizable before they appear in our butcher's showcase wrapped in plastic, or on our plates at the dinner table.

A lot of "culture" and "civilization" isolates us from this very real terror. We don't see the blood and mess of the preparation of our food (at least not most of us). We have learned how to avoid looking, and now it is difficult for many of us to see, even if we want to. Our consciousness has been lulled to sleep by pretty music and pretty packages. (Stand at the meat counter in your local supermarket and notice what kind of music you hear; it's probably not Beethoven.) Our sophisticated language covers over the pain in our lives by removing us from the directness of its imagery: the butcher is now the "meat manager."

Because we have been so isolated from all this earthiness, we have begun to think that we are not earthy and that our lives should be painless and terror-less. When pain confronts us we want to escape (with drugs or alcohol) or withdraw (into easy listening). What the earth and its music teach us is that pain is part of living, light is part of darkness, and day is meaningful because it moves into night. Painful moments are opportunities for waking up to life, allowing our hard shells to be broken so that new life can work at us and in us. But when we squash down the pain, it doesn't go away. It will gather and grow and then surprise us by erupting when we don't expect it and can't understand it because it has been glossed over, ignored, trivialized, and "forgotten." Its recognition will be further delayed by pain from other unprocessed experiences.

Ritual should help us to process life, to face its pain, and take the opportunity it offers to grow more deeply into life's mystery. Like music, ritual is not all easy-listening. It too remembers, respects, and even celebrates life's terror and darkness. We have now approached the reason for saying that music "is" ritual. Both participate in the fabric of life, both reveal and help us to acknowledge life in its joy and grief, understanding and confusion, yes and no. Music and ritual work so closely that they are one fabric.

Before proceeding further, we need a working definition for ritual, since the word has been used in many different ways.

Ritual is:

—a formal way of acknowledging and naming, communicating with and participating in,

—an event that life presents to us.

The first piece of our definition says that ritual is "formal," in the sense of conscious and chosen. One does not fall into ritual. Rather, one realizes that a moment of ritual is at hand and makes a choice to participate. Ritual is also formal because it has a plan, a shape, an organic flow. The form may be repetitive and will include gestures and symbols. Second, ritual allows us to acknowledge something that is happening in our lives (birth, death, transition of life style) so as not to miss what life presents. Further, ritual helps us to give the event a name, or to formalize our naming of what is happening. The naming gives us power-with the event. As we have already noted, if we are awake to life we won't feel powerless when life presents its light or darkness to us. Rather, our healthy stance is to greet life and work with it and learn from what it offers us. Naming, contrary to some interpretations, does not mean power-over, as for example in the Hebrew Book of Genesis when the earth creature names the animals. Naming a child does not mean having power over the child, but sharing your own life-power with her, inviting her into life. A name is something we grow into and something that grows with us. Naming what is happening in our lives enables us not to be frightened but to move on to the next task, which is communication. Perhaps by talking it through, drawing it, or dancing it we begin to learn what the event means. This communicating allows us to participate actively rather than stand on the side of life and just watch. The symbols and gestures assist in our participation so that we engage more than just our minds.

This definition of ritual reveals that rituals are created out of life experience because we don't want to miss anything, or to let go by a chance to connect with life's mysteries. Ritual moments emerge in our life and help us to cherish it and acknowledge its rich meaning. To test this definition of ritual, we will consider the ritual of a funeral. Often the death of a family member or a friend occurs in the unfamiliar environment of a hospital. Although hospital care often eases the difficulties of illness and dying, it also initiates the separation which will be the strongest impact of death.[3] The moment of a friend's death is one of the most sacred in human experience, since it seems that we too are standing on the threshold of life. Yet spending time in that special and mysterious presence is not allowed. The next time we see "the body" is at the funeral home, where every attempt is made to make the person look alive and only asleep. (This is true especially of women who are laid out in nightgowns, whereas men are usually in formal suits.) Funeral homes, caskets, limousines, and visiting hours are supposed to "ease the pain." Often, however, they do not give us the space and time to acknowledge and name the loss. We are held off from really seeing and feeling what is happening. This effect is enhanced by going to the cemetery but not to the grave, not ever seeing the hole, not touching the earth which will welcome its child again.

In the transition between the funeral home and cemetery some families go to church for a funeral ritual. It seems clear that church is the space in which naming and acknowledging ought to happen. Too often the church presents only the "light" side of death, the "new and eternal life" which the person who has died has now attained, although giving little assistance to those who are trying to communicate with the darkness of this event. In Roman Catholic liturgy we have lifted the pall of "Dies Irae" and have moved totally into the light of Alleluias and resurrection. The question we must ask here is: Who is the ritual for anyway? Too often we know people who have not dealt with death; their grief and anger burn in them and keep them in its bondage. Somehow the funeral rite should help us into the event, not in any morbid sense (death having power over us) but in an honest (power-with) sense. We can learn from death—about the universe and its rhythm, about ourselves, about God. The ritual can be a powerful moment of learning, naming, and celebrating.

Planning a ritual this rich is an awesome task. One of the questions that surfaces is: How much is enough without being too much? A word that will help us is "elegant"; a ritual should be elegant, in the first meaning of the word. Elegant comes from the Latin "eligere," which means to choose, to select. The symbols and gestures of the ritual should be carefully chosen; nothing should be there that is not chosen. Superfluous things (prayers, decorations, and the like) should not distract us. Elegant has a flavor of "just right," when you feel that nothing more can be taken away. Often our rituals are cluttered with spare parts that jangle in our heads and keep us from experiencing the real power of the ritual. In planning we select, adding only what is needed, what is essential. Who can better help us in this task than artists, whose lives are spent pruning and paring, sensing balance and relationship, repetition and variety? What needs to be repeated so that things are connected? What are the symbols that are powerful enough to continue to present life to us, no matter who we are or how old we are?

Many Christian rituals still use the earth elements (for example, water and fire), although their usage is often minimal (a dribble of water rather than immersion, a charcoal grill flame rather than an outdoor bonfire). Sometimes it is proposed that what is needed are new symbols, since the ones we have don't work any more. Considering that the newest cosmic story underscores our partnership with these elements, a better explanation for the impotence of our symbols is that people have lost touch with their elementary origins. When we recover a feeling for the wonder of the fireball, the strength of wind and water, the richness and fertility of earth, then we will see and feel our symbols and gestures with new eyes, eyes awake to the cosmic dancing around us. (Maybe our churches should have gardens instead of bingo parlors and schools.)

In addition to the strong and wise repetition of symbols, ritual also needs variation. The year provides a stunning rhythm which is reflected in our personal rhythms (the spring of my life, the winter of my life). Music participates in this variation by creating "seasoning" in ritual, darkness and light, major and minor, fast and slow, sound and silence. Within those myriad variations, music can be varied in its performance so that a well-known tune becomes fresh, or a new shadow is recognized in an ancient message. Music can provide repetition and variation in ritual because it *is* repetition and variation. It is the time and pace in which the ritual has flavor, texture, and wonderfully deep visions. [4]

If we feel that ritual is boring, what can we discover to be missing? What is it that William Dean (in this chapter's opening quote) and scores of young and not-so-young drop-outs want in ritual? It's not just "life" or "joy" or even measurable enthusiasm. Many churches are mistaken in thinking that providing up-beat music will swell attendance. Joyful, exuberant music is only half the story. The music of grief and pain must also be heard. What we are missing is passion. Our music is missing it, our assemblies and our ministers don't have it, our prayers and our gestures are languishing for it. We have valued solemnity and subdued color, music and language, and then blamed "the ritual" for being boring. A ritual can be boring, but any ritual not activated by and reflective of passionate living will be dry and unconnected. We can begin by redeeming the word passion from the pornographers who hold it hostage. They began using it when the churches stopped. We will come alive in church not by trying to inject passion into our ritual, but by living passionately, recapturing our earthy style, by letting go of our ladder-climbing preoccupations and joining in the circles of cosmic life. Then we can bring that vigor and that dancing to ritual, which may need to be re-shaped, indeed, but not because someone said it's better or "more alive" or "more faithful to our oldest traditions" but because we trust ourselves to claim the ritual and make it work for us, now.

This may mean that a lot of music and prayers (word-banners and artificial flowers for sure) will have to be let go, not because we were "wrong" or because they were "bad" (except plastic flowers; they're always bad) but because they don't work for us any more, they don't help us into life, into darkness and light, into mystery and wonder. We need an example. We have a good one in the text of a well-known, well-loved Christian hymn commonly used in rituals that celebrate the presence of the Holy Spirit.

Traditional Text	*Creation-Centered Text*
Come down, O Love divine,	Come round, O Love divine,
Seek thou this soul of mine,	Our love and trust refine,
And visit it with thine own	And visit us with your own
ardor glowing;	ardor glowing;
O Comforter, draw near,	O Comforter draw near,
Within my heart appear,	Within our lives appear,
And kindle it, thy holy flame	And kindle them, your holy
bestowing.	warmth bestowing.

O let it freely burn,
till earthly passions turn
To dust and ashes in its heat
    consuming;
And let thy glorious light

Shine ever on my sight,
And clothe me round the while
    my path illuming.

And so the yearning strong,
With which the soul will long,
Shall far outpass the power of
    human telling;
For none can guess its grace,
Till he becomes the place
Wherein the Holy Spirit makes
    His dwelling.

O let us freely burn
Till earthly passions turn
To works of justice, mercy,
    love renewing;
And let thy glorious light
    (night?)
Be for us pure delight
And clothe us round, the while
    our path creating.

And so the yearning strong
With which our hearts will long,
Shall far outpass the power of
    any telling;
For none can guess its grace,
Till we become the space
Wherein the Holy Spirit makes
    a dwelling.[5]

The strongest change in the text involves moving from a personal (me and my) context to the broader context of us and our, and a transformation of a theology that puts down earthly passions to one that celebrates and uses the power of that passion for doing good work. Although the text does not specifically broaden the scope to all creatures, the language does not exclude creatures other than humans. And the center of all those creatures is the heart—where warmth, longing, and grace find space to work their magic.

One of the most commonly heard complaints about our inability to spark life into ritual has to do with reluctant ministers, especially ministers who retain veto authority over the planning, or who still believe that it's their ritual (my Mass, my liturgy) as opposed to anyone else's. One frightening thing about this attitude is that it implies that some of us are more important than others at ritual, that some people have more ownership of it than others. Underlying this attitude is an attachment to a hierarchial image of ritual ministry in which we find our identity. I have to know who is above me and who is below me to know who I am. People simply cannot find their true identity in what they do, in any job, even if you call it ministry. People should know who thy are, and then choose to minister. Knowing who we are enables us to say,

"I want to minister," rather than "I feel called to minister." This latter statement is often a cover for what is really sought, which is the power that ministry (supposedly) gives. The power of ministry, like the power of music, is always power-with and never power-over. The power of ministry has to do with enabling people to live passionately, to rejoice in life's light and darkness, to be creative about working for the fullness of justice. Knowing who you are means understanding the rhythms of the life process, admitting weakness as well as strength, being humble (earthy) and trusting yourself and those with whom you live and work. Ministry is not trying to run people's lives or worry all night about whether or not they will make the right choice. Ministry is knowing yourself to be connected to those whom you serve and yet differentiated from them, whole and together as a human person, yet willing to be touched by others.

Part of knowing who you are is coming to the point of saying "I don't need anyone." Though this may sound like an angry statement, it is also a releasing one: once you can say "I don't need anyone," you can begin to freely love anyone. If you "need" someone, you may manipulate them to satisfy that need; consciously or unconsciously you are expecting things from that person. Coming to say "I don't need anyone" or "I don't need this situation (this job, this ministry)" allows you to choose it, love it, freely. On the other hand, if "you feel called" to the ministry, you may feel that you "need" to minister; and then you will feel guilty if the time comes when you can't or won't anymore. In religious life such people have "not persevered." In what have they not persevered? Really persevering in one's life, being passionate and creative, may mean realizing that certain spaces no longer have enough room to grow, or that certain life styles insulate us from life's passion. In this case persevering in "who you are" may mean making choices that affect what you do, choices that must be made out of wholeness and trust of ourselves.

The circle provides a good image for ministry at ritual. Movement in the circle is in and out rather than up or down. At the ministerial moment one steps into the circle to take care of the task at hand. When the task has been completed, one steps back out to join in the hand clasping which is the circle. Ministry happens because the ritual/the people have a task (leading prayer, making music, proclaiming holy words). Something needs to be done and someone steps forward (in) to do it. Ministry has nothing to do with being better or more holy or higher on the church ladder. It has a lot to do with being willing to dance with people.

It is not likely that ministry is going to get easier or simpler. Life on our planet is complex, and we cannot forget what we have learned and discovered as human species. The demands of ministry are likely to become even more strenuous as the planetary community wakes up to its task. Ministers must be people who are integrated and compassionate, who can suffer with others but not be consumed by them. The best image for such integration and compassion, such willingness to be present to, yet not manipulative and needy, is God. Perhaps this is the next "quantum leap" which the human species is being invited to take. Perhaps the darkness of disillusionment and burnt-out is the space of a great gestation, where humans will gather the energy for taking a new step in the evolution of our species.

> The human heart can go to the lengths of God.
> Dark and cold we may be, but this
> Is no winter now. The frozen misery
> Of centuries breaks, cracks, begins to move,
> The thunder is the thunder of the floes,
> The thaw, the flood, the upstart Spring.
> Thank God our time is now when wrong
> Comes up to face us everywhere,
> Never to leave us till we take
> The longest stride of soul men ever took.
> Affairs are now soul size.
> The enterprise
> Is exploration into God.[6]

More and more we hear about people "in transition." Far from being new ideas, change and growth are as old as the universe Transition in itself is not always indicative of wisdom, but transition based on trusting yourself and your life can encourage more in-depth living. Transitions are wonderful moments for ritual, for acknowledging and naming, participating in and communicating with the event that life presents to us. These rituals are not able to be determined chronologically (just because you're eighteen you are "grown-up") but rely on a reading of the right moment, the opportune time, when waiting is filled to overflowing into happening.

Such a ritual was needed for the recent closing of an old and wonderful house. It began with story-telling about the house and its many residents. Then a dance was begun, with people joining hands and moving through the house, including out the back door, into the street, and back in through the front door, all the while singing.

Sheila Carney   Cynthia Serjak

Com-ing and go-ing the en-er-gy flows. Wak-ing or rest-ing the house comes to know That life it en-cir-cles it al-so lets go.

The story-telling allowed the participants to formally ac-knowledge and name the importance of the house for its residents and visitors who found a welcome there. The dance enabled us to communicate with the house, by visiting

141

its external and internal spaces, and participate in the energy and warmth those spaces had provided. The ritual ended with Starhawk's chant:[7]

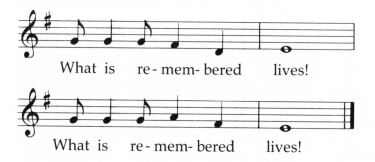

What is re-mem-bered lives!

What is re-mem-bered lives!

All present received buttons with the text of the chant printed on them, and the ritual dissolved into feasting on food, good conversation, and continued story-telling.

With music as our teacher and companion, we can look at how ritual works for us. Does it help us to name and celebrate our connection with the Creator and all of creation (hear and experience, begin a relationship)? Does it encourage us to enter the darknesses, the aloneness of life's pain (make us work hard, sometimes get frustrated, be led into the music, learn power-with)? Does it help us to trust ourselves, to be creative, to grow strong in our talents and convictions (to be co-creators)? Does it lead us back out to others to wake them up, to be compassionate and prophetic people, people whose life experience does not crush or burden them, but enables them to be strong, to unmask the fallacies of light-only Christianity, the mistrust and fear that religions perpetrate, the truly death-dealing sins of arrogance and apathy (make the music for others)? In particular, do rituals of healing really touch the pain and face the contradictions of life? Rituals that celebrate transition without facing the pain of separation no longer work for our lives. Perhaps people find rituals ineffective and boring not so much because they are not joyful enough, but because they are not willing to celebrate the darkness, and so their joy is hollow.

Like music, ritual is not meant to soothe or relax us, or make us feel good, but should connect and energize us. (How can this happen when we are all sitting in pews?) We all have a space in ritual, a time and a welcome; no one should feel useless or reluctant. The beginning of the ritual, the "gathering" time should establish this premise. Because of our connectedness in ritual, we can realize that we, whoever we are and whatever we do (constructive or destructive of life), will effect the continuing evolution of the universe. When the universe calls us into the dance, where will you be?

PART IV

Musicology for a New Creation

Introduction

This book began with an articulation of the lack of connectedness that exists among the various fields of human endeavor. In particular, we named the fields of science (multiple in themselves), theology, and the arts. We live in an age of intense specialization. Our point was to raise questions about what this specialization has done for and to humans, and then to see if there is any healing for our resulting disconnectedness. Music has been our vehicle, although there could be others. We explored the elements of music to uncover what power lies in them. We explored attitudes needed for quality music-making and saw that those attitudes have a lot in common with attitudes for global living. We played with the question of the global community being like a musical symphony, with incredibly rich and intricate weaving of voices. Delving even deeper, we celebrated the elements of the earth which we use in music-making or which inspire our music. We reflected on earth's music, its way of being, the elementary earth-song that is dialectical and dynamic rather than dualistic and static. Finally, we tried out the words of Jesus as earth wisdom and worked at a more universal hearing for the sayings of Christ. With the richness of the earth now opening up for us, we played with the origins of music, how it is "taught," and how it works for us in time, in personal development, and in ritual.

What is being proposed is that music has an important task, perhaps a more crucial task than ever before. Music is a powerful earth gift for revealing and re-presenting life to us, for helping us to enlarge our visions about what our lives can be. It is rich in lessons for global living, local decision-making, and personal growth. And yet much of music's power lies unevoked by many people. Often it is considered middle class, unavailable to the common person. Some "performers" are exploited and idolized, and become the heroes of a generation still starving for some good news about life.

Having determined that our problems lie in disconnectedness, and having suggested that music can be a metaphor for rediscovering our connections, it is time to come to some conclusions about how our healing is to occur. All things are connected. We are not talking about having to invent something new, nor are we arguing for a reversal of our life time or knowledge. Rather, we are asking that all of the ages of knowledge and wisdom be evoked now, among the first human people who are able to do that because of our common cosmic story, so that we can recover our origin-al connections and begin to circle in the cosmic dance. The word we will use to describe the reconnecting process is "return."

10

Returning Art and Artists to the People

What purpose, indeed, can music—or any form of art -
serve if it does not speak in a language that all can
understand?[1]

The music-making process can be a powerful metaphor
for personal living and working at global community. It is a
creative process which does not resist the darkness and
mystery of its content, but cherishes and celebrates sound
and silence, light *and* darkness, consonant *and* dissonant
harmony. Its co-creative effort results in music which is
sung, played, or danced again and anew. In the process the
artist learns to have power with the material at hand.
Composers will often speak of not really knowing where an
idea comes from or how it is heard inside them. Others will
describe an impulse to laugh at what has occurred through
them in the creative process.[2] This is akin to the divine
laughter which must have accompanied the spinning out of
the great fireball of creation. In the music-making process
the artist learns to trust herself or himself, and out of that
trust are born new sounds, new images, and new music.

What an incredible message this music has for a people
who fear darkness and pain, who want to dispel all mystery
from life, who are plugged up and bored, who see no reason
to participate in the ongoing creation of the earth. Music
introduces us to the pleasure and excitement of being caught
by a gift of the universe. It reconnects us to an energy for
falling in love again, for participating in the universe, and
therefore working to save and savor it. Among the people to
whom musicians should be returning are people who are

working for social justice. The laughter of creation needs to be heard in the picket line and the protest march. For it is the energy of laughter that allows us to let go of our fear of the darkness and enter into the risk of co-creation.

We have recognized that music-making is a helpful metaphor for personal and global living. Is there any connection between music-making and personal and global spirituality? More critically, is there a theology that welcomes artists?

In his "Primer in Creation Spirituality," *Original Blessing*, theologian Matthew Fox names four paths appropriate to this ancient and earthy theology.

Via Positiva:	Befriending Creation
Via Negativa:	Befriending Darkness, Letting Go and Letting Be
Via Creativa:	Befriending Creativity, Befriending Our Divinity
Via Transformativa:	Befriending the New Creation, Compassion and Justice

What we find here are the same dynamic movements that we have discovered as parts of the music-making process: the initial engagement, the struggle with mystery and darkness, co-creation, and sharing of the new creation with others. Here is a spirituality that shares the same underlying dynamic as music. Fox's articulation of the four paths enables artists to find a welcome in theology. To further enhance this possibility, he names as one of the themes in the third path "Art as Meditation" and another "Faith as Trust of Images" and still another "How Our Lives as Works of Art Spiral Beauty Back into the World." Imagine a theology which celebrates art as a means of relationship to our divine center. Imagine a theology which returns art and artist to people who are working at the "religious" development of the human species.

148

What churches need to do now to renew self and society is to take spirituality seriously; this means taking art seriously. Not art for the sake of art; not art for the sake of making banners or teapots; not art for sale. But art as prayer, art as meditation. Only art as meditation allows one to let go of art as production à la capitalism and return to art as process, which is the spiritual experience that creativity is about. Only art as meditation reminds people so that they will never forget that the most beautiful thing a potter produces is . . . the potter.[3]

Here we discover where the dynamic of the art process is heading: to and through the creation of the art (the music) to the creation and re-creation of the person in whose hands the art takes shape. Music is for people, for their pleasure and conversion, for their re-creation and transformation. Music for easy listening is a severe deflation and an utter travesty of music's true power. Like so many other gifts from the universe, music has been squished into production categories, stripped of its speaking power, and prostituted for the sake of gain (success, money, stardom, and the like). The human body needs to be reclaimed from pornographers; music needs to be redeemed from those who have betrayed its power, in whose hands it has become merely entertainment. Artists must return even to those people who oppress and control them, and work with them to restore the integrity of their art.

There is a serious heresy abroad in the land. It preaches that artists are strange people, hard to get along with, dangerous, irresponsible, inconsistent. There may be some truth to these accusations at a superficial level; but perhaps artists are simply living up to what we expect of them. We have made them elitist, set them apart from us because we shun being creative and so artists make us feel inept. Artists trust themselves, learn radical trust in their own images, and this makes them seem arrogant to the rest of us who are afraid of faith in ourselves. They are not bound by clock time, and that makes them "irresponsible" in the eyes of people whose master is the clock. Artists are always straining to see the other side, keeping the door open while others want to close it; this makes them seem stubborn and inconsistent.

If artists have been content to be separate from us, someone needs to initiate their return to the community so that their precious learning and wisdom about art's process (demands and joys) can unmask the fallacy of this heresy we have heard for much too long. Artists may be reluctant to expose themselves to the fray, to the great masses of humanity who want to ogle them and make them gods. And so everyone has to realize that artists are people too; in fact, in the broader sense of time, they are people before they are artists. Like everyone else, artists have to work at what allures them, what wants to be born in them, what connects and energizes them for living.

One of the community's serious responsibilities is to free artists to do art. Too many of them are working at jobs which do not suit them and do not engage their talent. This sad situation results because artists are unable to make a living doing art. A musician must eat, be sheltered and clothed, perhaps provide for a family, just like any other member of the community. This means adequate pay for work. But there are not many musicians who can play music for a living. Some fortunate few attain the status of concert artists and live an exhausting life on the road. A few others are able to manage by playing and teaching. But many, many others must supplement their meager income by serving in administrative roles, arts management, or working for the telephone company. The situation gets even worse when one looks at statistics for church musicians.

We expect artists to work double-time, to work at a "regular" job and do art on the side, in their "free" time. If we all shared in art processes (gardening, sewing, painting, working with clay) not to produce art, but to be part of it, to learn from it, to be shaped by it, we would celebrate the artists in our communities in a much healthier way. Rather than displaying them on pedestals or hiding them in garrets, we would sit them in our midst and allow their creative energy to warm our daily lives. We would also acknowledge that art is hard work, that it gets us dirty and sometimes reveals to us things we would rather not see.

A person who works with clay will find that a tendency to control the clay will not enable the clay to "work." One must learn power *with* the clay, working *with* the clay to see what will be co-created. A person who approaches the clay wanting to control it may realize in this process that he approaches other things in the same way. Thus the clay becomes the opportunity to learn about life. This may be hard work and involve a difficult conversion. [4] In this story the first product of the process is something new in the person. The clay product may not be beautiful or meaningful to anyone else, but it will be a powerful reminder to the person who made it of the conversion the clay invoked. The "professional" artist in this scenario is the one who stands by, perhaps encouraging the letting go and working with, as the worker struggles to know the process. The artist is experienced in the process and trusts it, knowing that the darkness of letting go may be very frightening. There is no way to avoid it, and the clay will insure that. Having someone there to listen to the fear and encourage the patience and perseverance while finding one's own way will facilitate the learning. The best piano teacher is the one whose vision of the Beethoven sonata is so alluring that the student will be motivated to begin the finger exercises and to spend the hours of practice in co-creation.

The other problem which surfaces in our wanting artists to be able to make a living at doing art is the exorbitant cost of being a listener at a live performance. Live musical experiences cost more than the average person can pay. While working for just compensation, artists must not forget the numbers of people who no longer can afford to come to hear them make music. The implication is that live musical concerts are for only middle and upper class folks. This enhances an already prevalent attitude that art cannot even be understood by the common person and is not "for" everyone. If artists and art are to be returned to the people, the return must be to all the people.

Another aspect of the artist's work (or those who support artists) concerns confronting systems that belittle the importance of quality in art and any other kind of work. Consumerism can be as dreadful a plague in art as anywhere else. The worry to meet a demand by producing more and more is foreign to the flow of a healthy spirituality. People may spend much money and energy to have "the latest by the latest," just as religious consumers may think that by stockpiling "grace" or multiplying prayers they will have a higher (on the ladder again) place in heaven. Difficult as it may be, the artist must return even to the market place and the churches to expose the fallacies of consumerism. By refusing to submit to its pressure an artist (and an observer/listener) reaffirms the value of connecting to life's own dynamic flow as it is revealed in the artistic and life processes. This problem is too immense to be addressed only by artists. They must be assisted in getting off the ladder by those who value what they do.

A particular problem here has to do with the availability of reproduction equipment. This relatively new field (in the history of the planet and its music) affects the visual arts (prints, copies, plates in books) as well as the musical world where records, tapes, and compact discs make music available to the consumer "on the market." (For the moment we are talking about legal and compensated reproduction.) The positive side to this technological reality is that a wide range of people who might not otherwise hear music can be exposed to the world's largest orchestras playing in the world's finest acoustics and being led by the world's most famous conductors. Something still is missing, however, and that is the irreplaceable magic that happens between the performer and listener in the live performance (or the magic between the observer and a piece of art). As we have said, the most important product in the artistic process is the person, in this case the performer and the listener. Nothing can reproduce the vitality of a live performance which is always enhanced by the visual spectacle. There is something definitely "in the air," some charged energy that makes the live performance the most captivating experience.

Although musical reproduction engages a wider audience, it also provides more secure income for the composer/performer. The temptations of this security may lead even the best artists into the consumerist trap. A performer can become an overnight success because of reproduction possibilities. The temptation is to take advantage of the success, since in this game success is usually short-lived. To take advantage means to provide a constant response of new material, to sell out quality to the demand of quantity. It is no wonder that many of the superstars are unable to handle the intense darkness that moves in after stardom has passed. Although our best examples come from the popular music world, they can also be found in serious music and even, increasingly, in the church music field. Churches should be especially careful not to fall into the same snare by making heroes out of their young artists and exhausting them through demands for new music and coast-to-coast appearances.

Of great concern, of course, is the illegal and uncompensated reproduction of material, on cassette tapes, VCRs, and copy machines. In light of our previous discussion about freeing the artist to do work and not wanting to exploit their talent, it should be obvious that such reproductions are in fact "immoral" as well as illegal. Again we recognize that some of the greatest offenders in this area are churches. Because they refuse to give adequate budgets to the music program, churches indirectly but effectively encourage their musicians to make scores available to their choirs through illegal reproductions. Because the artist/composer is not local, it may be hard for churches to see the result of this short-sightedness. If the starving artist worked down the street, perhaps we would be more aware of how easily we exploit them and how responsible we are to them for their state.

The ultimate tool of the consumerist economy is advertising. Again, many people who want to be serious artists find financial stability by supplying music and artwork for advertising companies. An artist who reflects on the implications of this work has some serious choices to make about the integrity of participating in such manipulative endeavors. Our economy is based on the efficacy of advertizing; our spending is manipulated by fad and fancy. Artists (and others concerned with the quality of our lives) must begin to raise questions about what is really valuable to us, what we wish to pass on to the generations that will (hopefully) follow us.

There are many ways in which all of us can begin to

address the conditions that prevent artists from returning to the people. Making choices within the context of the whole story rather than the smaller more shortsighted context of immediate satisfaction or gain, will strengthen us in the long run. Standing free of consumerism may not seem to have significant impact on the business ethic, but it will have an effect on us and those around us, and the energy for wiser choices will grow.

> Integrity means consistency; we act in accordance with our thoughts, our images, our speeches; we keep our commitments. Power-over can be wielded without integrity, but power-from-within cannot. For power-from-within is the power to direct energy—and energy is directed by images in our minds and speech as well as by our actions. If these are consistent, energy flows freely in the direction we choose and we have power. If what we do is at odds with what we say or think, then energy gets blocked or mis-channeled. If I think and say that I hate pollution, and yet walk by and leave beer cans lying at my feet, the energy of my feelings is dissipated. Instead of feeling my own power to do something, however small, about litter, I feel and become more powerless.[5]

This thoughtful analysis brings to mind other comparable situations: the dieter who "cheats" and then must work doubly hard to restore the determination to persevere; the social justice preacher whose choir sings from illegally made copies; pro-life anti-abortionists who ignore or even support war-making. There is no longer a place to say "What I do doesn't matter." Everything we do matters. We must choose in which direction the "mattering" happens. Aside from the long-range effects of our doing nothing, there is an immediate loss of the flow of our energy for good work. We compromise our values and divert our power for firm commitment.

Another area which can be helpful in addressing the return of artists to the people is education. Unfortunately we are living in a time when music and art programs are still being cut from curricula rather than being strengthened.

Again our drive for specialization has affected even our most primary educational experiences. If we don't "choose" art or music as a career, our exposure to it is limited to pleasure and leisure time. We lose touch with the power of the arts in our lives and the wisdom of the artistic process for our growth. In asking that art and the artist be returned to the people we are acknowledging the value of what the artists may produce for us, but more importantly, of what the artists are for us and what we can learn from them.

11

Returning Mysticism and Prophecy to Spirituality

The creation-centered spiritual tradition considers *com-passion* rather than *contemplation* as the fulfillment of the spiritual journey that takes one back to one's origins in renewed ways. It considers justice to be absolutely integral to the spiritual journey.[1]

An analogy can be drawn between the return of the artist to the community and the return of the mystic to spirituality and the churches. Our ideas about mystics range from weird navel-gazers to sappy, sentimental holy cards of virgins and martyrs. Just as art needs to be reopened to everyone, so mysticism needs to be brought back into the center of life. If we reflect on the music-making process we recognize that the experience is often one of being "out of control" in the sense of being so caught by the music, of being so absorbed in the work, that one loses track of the passage of time. In this out-of-time experience the musician has a chance to dialogue with the music, to learn power with it, to be drawn into its mystery, and to have visions and new insights.

What better description of a mystical experience could we want? The partner need not be music; it could be clay, or a garden, a sunset, a cave, even a storm. The freedom of mysticism is in the letting go, allowing oneself to be caught and embraced but not consumed by what is Other, to be awestruck at beauty and power, to let go of controlling the Other or our relationship. We can fall in love with things as well as people if our temptations to human arrogance are healed by a cosmic understanding of our connectedness. Mysticism allows us to open our eyes to what is really going on around us. With this new energy moving in us we are not afraid to let go of being so oppressed by what we have to do, and so can be freed to be who we are, which is the most important growing a human person can do. The mystical experience is a freeing and energizing one. Then we must ask the question: Where does the energy born in mysticism go? The answer is: Into prophecy.

The vision evoked in us of our connectedness with all creation energizes us to work for the fulfillment of this vision in the lives of all creatures and in the very life systems of the planet. It energizes us to wake up others to institutions that oppress and check the flow of life, to speak out about the contradiction in our values and our way of life. The musician's vision of the finished work energizes her to do the painstaking work of writing out note after note, finding a publisher, poring over galleys and corrections, patiently waiting for the fulfillment of the vision. Encouragement to work at and understand the vision and its fulfillment comes to us from ancient writing, from the Hebrew prophet Habakkuk.

> Write down the vision clearly upon the tablets,
> so that one can read it readily.

> For the vision still has its time,
> presses on to fulfillment,
> and will not disappoint;

> If it delays, wait for it,
> it will surely come, it will not be late.[2]

This wisdom confirms our sense that things happen when it's time for them to happen: the tomato is ripe when the tomato is ripe; the painting is finished when the painting is finished; the vision is fulfilled when the vision is fulfilled.

Mysticism is being reclaimed because we are hungry for visions and running dangerously low on energy. Many forms of mysticism are being recovered from Eastern traditions. It is wondrous that just when the distance between the East and West is being narrowed by travel and communications technology, we are so much in need of an exchange of wisdom between East and West. However, simply adopting Eastern prayer modes is not enough. We in the West must work to combine Eastern wisdom and discipline with the best Western desire to get things done, to work for the survival of the planet, to free all people and creatures to join in the cosmic dancing. Our mysticism is not for self-salvation or self-protection. It is for nourishment and inspiration to work and prophesy. It uncovers for us new sources of energy with which we can cooperate so that we can throw off our apathy and boredom and be prophets of cosmic living.

Let us pause to reflect on a mystical experience with music. We have said that music in its best form does not lull us to sleep, but in fact, wakes us up. In its harmony we not only find peace and integration, we also find tension and dissonance. The vision that music offers us reveals that life holds peace as well as conflict, integration as well as dis-integration. This vision is not dull or easy to deal with; it challenges us—all of us—to open our thinking about living life in its best form. Out of the visions of our music-making we come to prophesy about life; out of the strength of its energy we sustain our work on the planet. Finally, we are now able to see that making music is about making justice.

Because music and justice are woven of the same fabric, music-making is an evolutionary activity, some would say a revolutionary one, still others a dangerous one. If the visions of music are allowed to be heard, we won't be satisfied until they are offered to all of creation. If the mystical visions of justice-makers are seen in the land, no one will rest until they are accomplished for all creatures. Imagine what would happen if all people became mystics and prophets—what a new creation we would be. Mysticism, like music, like all art, like all good work, should be available to all of us. Our spirituality has been stale and diluted and privatized. All the excitement of vision-seeking and connecting has been dis-persed into worrying about being sinful. It is time to return mysticism to our churches, to teach our children that being mystical is not being weird but is being fully human.

What seems clear is that the people who are most ready for this message are the people who have nothing to lose,

159

those who have less baggage to worry about. Could this be the newest (or most ancient) meaning of the words "Blessed are the poor in spirit; theirs is the kingdom of heaven"? If, in fact, God's reign is among us, could it be that the poor are the first who are likely to see it because they don't have the luxury of being able to be distracted by how much they own and what they must do to take care of it? Are not those oppressed by racism and sexism the most likely candidates for the message that "who you are" is much more important than "what you have"?

Artists must be returned to the center of the community so that their lessons about being human can be heard. So also the poor among us must not be relegated to the edges or the ghettos, but should live in our midst and teach us about freedom and mysticism. When Jesus said, "leave all that you have and follow me," he was not saying, "just be carefree and trust God." More likely he was saying, "if you want visions, if you want to be a prophet, you must let go of what might distract you, you must empty your arms and your life so that the truth of creation can come pouring in."

By contrast, those who have much to lose in the face of this message will be the ones who will not be able to hear it. Having isolated themselves from life's offers of mystery and darkness, they are out of practice at letting go; in fact they are practiced in holding on, in being in control, in having power over things and people. They are not able to see the vision because their eyes are worried over bank statements and security systems. When traveling they have so much baggage to worry about that they miss the scenery and the native flavor. Life is too short to risk missing what's happening because so many "things" demand your attention. It's much better to travel in old clothes, which won't mind the dusty train rides, than to buy new clothes and worry for their protection. It's much more fun to have little baggage and be freer to move and be spontaneous than to lose those opportunities because of cumbersome luggage. Blessed are those who are poor, who can travel lightly, who are able to see and see clearly.

One of the techniques of classical spirituality has been asceticism. The technique for a spirituality that welcomes the artists and the poor and oppressed will be discipline. Some forms of asceticism may be helpful if one is wealthy enough to afford to choose what things to "give up." Many people, for example, do not have the "luxury" of choosing when to fast—they fast all the time because they have little to eat. But our best teacher will be in the discipline of the activity that engages us. It is our vision of the sound of the anthem that will discipline us to learn it. It is the vision of a rich harvest that disciplines us to get into the garden and get earthy (dirty). It will be the vision of a church that celebrates the light and darkness of life's flow that will free us from our narrow minded pews and prayerbooks so that we may dance around the altar.[3]

12

Returning Beauty to the Cosmos

The outward work
will never be puny
if the inward work
is great.
And the outward work
can never be great or even good
if the inward one is puny or of little worth.
The inward work invariably
includes in itself
all expansiveness,
all breadth,
all length,
all depth.
Such a work
receives and draws all its being
from nowhere else except
from and in the heart of God.[1]

The new story of the cosmos provides a new cosmology, a
new way for us to think about how the universe began and
continues in existence. This cosmology includes serious
interpretations for the life of the human species. But we also
need a theology that is willing to deal with the implications of
this scientific data, dialogue with it, not in any way to try to
define or answer it, but to connect it to our understandings
about who God is and what the activity of creation means.
People are looking for a spirituality that addresses the
cosmos, that respects and celebrates it. Creation-centered
theology is very old and very new. It draws on the most
primal revelations of the divine, the most classical forms of
spirituality, and the newest understandings of science. One

of its strongest themes is the meaning of and motivation for human participation in the on-going creation of the universe. Or, to put it another way, it recognizes that our dreams and hopes for a world of justice are the universe working in us, and that our richest source of energy for seeing those dreams through to fulfillment is the universe itself.

Creation-centered theology is not afraid to face the darkness in this project. It recognizes "the fall" and the imperfection as real, but also as a potential for enormous human growth. It embraces a dialectical mode of living, and it welcomes in a special way those who are on the fringes of the old world view. It offers itself as a mature and responsible partner to science and the arts, so that the circling dialogue that can now occur opens up all of life, including religion and spirituality, to a healthy universe-al context. In this context, what we need is less a theology of music-making than a revitalized musicology that is also worthy and eager to be a partner in envisioning a future for the planet and its newest child, the human species.

The field of musicology encompasses a study of history and interpretation of music. Like our thinking about theologians and scientists, our picturing of musicologists has included bespectacled and serious looking people (usually men) surrounded by stacks of musical scores and volumes of music history, who teach music as an academic subject, generally of interest only to other musicologists. This new musicology (like the "new" theology) takes into account data about the science of music-making in the context of an emerging cosmology where all the fields of human endeavor have a place in the dialogue. It also knows (like the new cosmology) the latest ventures in theology and theology's interest in music and ritual. But it does not hesitate to trust its own images (music as ritual) and work at its own development as an independent art. Let us work through some specific themes that might emerge in this new musicology. The new musicology will:

1. acknowledge and celebrate its cosmic connections;

2. offer its own movement and dynamic as a model for global living, its process as a metaphor for life processes, and even its language (for example, rhythm, melody, harmony) as helpful in opening up images and symbols;

3. speak to a savoring and saving of the earth and its elements, since they are so essential to its own life;

4. reject triteness as well as fadism, music for sale and music as a commodity, music as background and musicians as only entertainers, music as drug or manipulation or escape;

5. address itself to other areas of life in a manner that invites cooperation and dialogue; it will be non-elitist and welcoming;

6. help the human population of the planet to return the incredible beauty of the planet earth to the cosmos.

Cosmic Connecting

Like many other fields of human endeavor, music has often been found to be turned inward, making music only for musicians. As with other fields, music is now invited to turn outward again, to greet the cosmos, recognize its own connectedness with the rest of life and its origin with that life in the fireball. This is not to imply that music will change or that new music must be written. Much of the music we already have is cosmic in proportion; we can hear it again and again and still not be satisfied or bored. This kind of music also has universe-al appeal, can be heard from country to country, and needs no translation. But there is also music that is not interested in cosmic connecting, music written or played for manipulation or separation. This is the music which must be called to task by musicians themselves as well as by others. Musicians must feel citizenship in the universe so that their music can work at connecting creatures rather than separating or dividing them. Responsible musicianship will mean speaking out about music's abuse as well as working to release its true power.

Music As Model and Metaphor

We resist the narrowness of thinking that music offers an ideal toward which the entire creation should strive. We cannot make music the saving grace or the answer to all our problems. We name the themes of music to see whether they reflect life and so can help us in dealing with life's problems. This naming strengthens what we have already discovered about the rhythm of our lives by offering yet another member to the dialogue which begins "life is like . . . " Music is a model in an organic way, since it shows us how things emerge, grow, develop, and come to fullness and completion. Music demonstrates without explaining, reveals with defining, offers suggestions without claiming to give answers.

As a metaphor, music can also be susceptible to limitations, but it offers a story which adds nuance to life's unfolding dynamic. It persuades us not to package our lives but to keep them fluid and open. The power of the metaphor confirms our determination to call musicians and other artists to return to the center of the community to tell their stories as well as to share the products of their art.

Perhaps most critically, the metaphor of the process of music-making helps us to answer the question: How can artists address the problems of social justice which are bringing our planet to the brink of self-destruction? In the face of a multifaced global crisis musicians may be tempted to stop the music to work more directly at the problems. And yet they are hesitant to do so, wondering why they can't make music and make justice as well. It is unfair, and now we can say cosmically unwise, to ask musicians to be inattentive to the talent within them. What we have discovered in exploring the process and attitudes of quality art is that music-making and justice-making are not unrelated works: in making music we are already making justice. We are announcing that injustice (lack of cooperation and respect, mistrust and suspicion) does not hold us in bondage. In our own music-making bodies we show that cooperation and reverence, trust and humility are alive and well and available to us. Our difficulty is that the power of this message has been co-opted because the power of music-making has been dispersed and the musicians removed from the center of life. The justice inherent in the music-making is like a great secret waiting to be revealed, a watershed of energy and vision that needs to be released now. The good news is that musicians should keep doing what they're doing, but do it better and more out in the open, with more attention to letting the message of the music be heard. This will require very creative and courageous musicians, artists who are willing to play within and around the context of the contemporary struggle of the planet to survive, teachers who will invite their students not only into the notes, but into the life in which the notes were conceived, born, and continue to live. Some people ask how in the midst of the turmoil which surrounds us, people can continue to play and sing. They play and sing not because they wish to be distracted, but because they know that in the very act of playing and singing they are already announcing that the turmoil will not ultimately prevail. In the music-making they are already weaving justice, choosing to affirm a quality life for all people; they are already making the music of the new creation.

Music and the Earth

In returning to the center of the community, musicians also recognize their humility, their earthiness—that in their music-making they are playing out their gratitude to the Earth for having conceived and nourished the sound which humans have named music. Though gratitude may be the initial reason, musicians grow into a more mature relationship of mutual respect and cooperation with Earth. Even more wonderfully, they fall in love with Earth, fascinated by its primal rhythms, intoxicated by its intensely colored melodies, embraced and surrounded by its continually and infinitely unfolding harmonies. Once they have felt the depth of this relationship, musicians can do nothing else but work to save the Earth and to call others to get their feet back on the ground, even to remove their shoes and once again feel the sacred soil beneath their feet. Music does not wish to provide an escape from the Earth, but to invite us more deeply into its richness and mystery. When people are in love they can do incredible things for one another. Imagine what could happen if we all fell in love again—with Earth, with its gifts, with its justice—and started making all kinds of music for the great and enticing Earth-dance!

Integrity in Music Making

Musicians who rediscover the crucial message of their art will begin to refuse to be the tool of consumerism or nationalism or any other -ism. They will stand and work for integrity in their own art and wake up others to do so in their own lives and work. They will refuse to play and sing music that is trite or fadish, music that may sell quickly and widely but that glosses over and weakens the rhythm of life, that belittles love, that implies there is no darkness in life, that is sentimental and deluded about life. They will stop the background music which follows us everywhere and invite people into silence or conversation. They will no longer allow entertainment to be music's only role, or escape to be its only message. This is far from an easy task. Musicians will have to join with others who are already working at uncovering these kinds of unworthy and unwelcome uses of earth's gifts. They, too, must get off the ladder that being successful offers, and enter the circle of living in integrity and healthy pride.

Cooperation and Dialogue

In this ever-widening circle of friends who each contribute unique talents and skills, there will emerge a new and exciting dialogue, based not on a need to compete or control,

168

but on a wonder at the richness of the human venture, the beauty of its foibles as well as its strong points. The conversation will be non-elitist and welcoming to all, regardless of their work. It will extend its listening to non-two-legged creatures, even to the Earth itself. The dialogue will not always be verbal—it may be in symbol and gesture, music and art, photography and painting, choreography and mime. No human venture will be better or more celebrated, and the only ones excluded will be those that deal death. All will recognize the cooperation at the heart of this new creation. Its first children will be the people themselves, those who give new life to themselves as they develop their own images, ideas, and rituals.

The Cosmic Response-Ability

This dialogue will be of cosmic proportion and consequence, since the universe cannot ignore its appearance and its significance. In fact the universe has been looking for it. As the old Chinese proverb says: "When a question is posed ceremoniously, the universe responds."[2] What the new cosmology proposes, and ancient Chinese wisdom knows, is that the universe has been waiting for this moment for billions of years, longing for the human species to take up its intended task: to wonder at and celebrate fully the immense and infinite beauty of the cosmos.[3] It is the ability and pleasure of the human species to reflect that beauty and so return it to the cosmos, not by being any less than human (by making war and destruction) but by being fully human (making friends and savoring). The signs are slowly and quietly appearing that the circling has begun. We still have a choice to enter or not enter, to let go of our ladders and join the circle or turn away from the hand that is offered. There is no doubt that the music is ready. *Now where are the musicians, please? We want to begin the dance.*

Notes

Part One

Chapter 1

1. Fritjof Capra, *The Tao of Physics* (Colorado: Shambala Publications, 1975) 192.

2. Mircea Eliade, *The Sacred and the Profane* (New York: Harcourt, Brace and World, Inc., 1959) 95.

3. "A Maori Cosmogony," trans., Hare Hongi, *The Journal of the Polynesian Society*, no. 63 (September 1907) 113ff. Quoted in Charles H. Long, *Alpha: The Myths of Creation* (New York: George Braziller, 1963) 172.

4. This passage about the cosmological story is taken from *The Universe Is a Green Dragon: A Cosmic Creation Story* by Brian Swimme (Santa Fe: Bear and Company, 1985) 27 and 28. Written as a dialogue between two speakers, this book relates the story of the creative energy in all matter and in the particular creative task of the human species. If the New Story is news to you, this book is an excellent place to begin your cosmic reading.

5. Ibid. 27.

6. *The Fate of the Earth* by Jonathan Schell (New York: Kopf, 1982) is an excellent and very readable book exploring this topic, which the author calls "The Second Death."

7. See Alfred North Whitehead, *Science and the Modern World* (New York: MacMillan Company, 1954), Chapter XII, "Religion and Science."

8. Later we shall elaborate on the connections between the artistic process and life projects, and how art can teach us about living well.

9. For a discussion of the many kinds of ecstasy waiting for us, see Matthew Fox, *Whee! We, Wee, All the Way Home: A Guide to Sensual Prophetic Spirituality* (Santa Fe: Bear and Company, 1980).

10. See *Black Elk Speaks* (New York: Pocket Books, 1972; originally William Morrow and Co., 1932) for many stories of vision-seeking and the importance of ritual.

11. *Life with Picasso* by Francoise Gilot and Carlton Lake (New York: McGraw Hill, Inc., 1964) tells an interesting story of the life of a popular artist and the demands of maintaining a hero's life.

12. Matthew Fox, *Meditations with Meister Eckhart* (Santa Fe: Bear and Company, 1983) 14.

13. Gabriele Uhlein, *Meditations with Hildegard of Bingen* (Santa Fe: Bear and Company, 1983) 48.

14. The study of mystics like Hildegard and Eckhart and of the New Story of the cosmos, is happening in places like the Institute in Culture and Creation Spirituality (ICCS) in Oakland, California. The program includes art as meditation courses, which open up the richness of the artistic process to students and teachers alike. A relative of ICCS is Friends of Creation Spirituality, a group which publishes *Creation* magazine and supports efforts in interdisciplinary communication.

15. Carolyn Merchant, *The Death of Nature: Women, Ecology and the Scientific Revolution* (San Francisco: Harper and Row, 1980) 42.

16. Wendell Berry connects our lack of appreciation for the wonder of our bodies to our lack of concern for the earth from whence we came. "While we live our bodies are moving particles of the earth, joined inextricably both to the soil and to the bodies of other living creatures. It is hardly surprising, then, that there should be some profound resemblances between our treatment of our bodies and our treatment of the earth." *The Unsettling of America: Culture and Agriculture* (San Francisco: Sierra Club Books, 1977) 97.

17. See Chapter Seven, "We're All Healers" in Margo Adair's *Working Inside Out, Tools for Change* (Berkeley: Wingbow Press, 1986).

Chapter 2

1. Brian Swimme and Matthew Fox, *Manifesto for a Global Civilization* (Santa Fe: Bear and Company, 1982) 11-12.

2. *Nicene and Post-Nicene Fathers*, vol. 4, ed. by Philip Schaff, Henry Wace, and others (New York: The Christian Literature Company, 1892) 24.

3. From Robert Bly, *The Kabir Book* (Boston: Beacon Press, 1977) 35.

4. Susan Woodruff, *Meditations with Mechtild of Magdeburg* (Santa Fe: Bear and Company, 1982) 87.

5. J. R. Tolkein, *Silmarillion* (Boston: Houghton Mifflin, 1977) 15, 17.

6. Some of the ideas in the following description of the elements of music were first developed in a talk given at the National Association of Pastoral Musicians Regional Convention in Cleveland, Ohio (June 1984) and later published in *Pastoral Music* 9:2 (December-January 1985) 23-29.

7. Capra, *The Tao* 244.

8. For an interesting and informative discussion of the effect of poetic meter in song, see Austin Lovelace, *The Anatomy of Hymnody* (Chicago: GIA Publications, Inc., 1965).

9. Hildegard, in Uhlein, *Meditations* 49.

10. Mechtild, in Woodruff, *Meditations* 50.

11. Bly, *The Kabir Book* 40.

12. Alfred North Whitehead, *Adventure of Ideas* (New York: MacMillan Company, 1933) 169.

13. T. S. Eliot, *The Four Quartets* (New York: Harcourt, Brace, Jovanovich, 1971) 44.

14. Fox and Swimme, *Manifesto* 12.

15. This question may be asked of various arts. See Annie Dillard, *Living by Fiction* (New York: Harper and Row, 1982), Part III "Does Art Have Meaning?," especially pages 173 and following.

16. Claude Samuel, *Conversations with Olivier Messiaen*, trans., Felix Apprahamian (London: Stainer and Bell, 1976) 12.

17. Ibid. 1.

18. Olivier Messiaen, *The Technique of My Musical Language*, trans., John Satterfield (Paris: Alphonse Leduc, 1956) 34.

19. Pierrette Mari, *Olivier Messiaen* (Paris: Editions Seghers, 1965) 54. I am grateful to Marie Immaculée Dana, R.S.M. for this translation.

20. Claude Samuel, *Conversations* 51.

21. The theme of royal personhood has been developed by Helen Kenik in "Toward a Biblical Basis for Creation Theology" in *Western Spirituality: Historical Roots, Ecumenical Roots*, ed., Matthew Fox (Santa Fe: Bear and Company, 1981) 27–75. The theme is also used by Matthew Fox in *Original Blessing: A Primer in Creation Spirituality* (Santa Fe: Bear and Company, 1983). See Theme 7. Also in *Breakthrough: Meister Eckhart's Creation Spirituality in New Translation*, introduction and commentary by Matthew Fox (New York: Doubleday, 1980). See Sermon Thirty-Six: "Everyone an Aristocrat, Everyone a Royal Person."

22. Pablo Casals, *Joys and Sorrows*, as told to Albert E. Kahn (New York: Simon and Schuster, 1970) 99.

23. Hildegard, in Uhlein, *Meditations* 59.

24. Eckhart, in Fox, *Meditations* 28.

25. Casals, *Joys* 295.

Part Two

Introduction

1. I learned this chant from Starhawk in her "Creating Rituals" class at the Institute in Culture and Creation Spirituality at Holy Name College, Oakland, California, fall semester 1985.

Chapter 3

1. Quoted on the back cover of *Creation* 1:4 (September/October 1985).

2. Archibald Rutledge, *Peace in the Heart* (Garden City: Doubleday, Doran and Co. Inc., 1930) 15.

3. This chant can be found with many others in Starhawk, *Dreaming the Dark* (Boston: Beacon Press, 1982) 223.

4. Starhawk, *The Spiral Dance* (San Francisco: Harper and Row, 1979) 202.

5. Brian Swimme, "Earth Fire," *Creation* 1:3 (July/August 1986) 9–10.

6. The *Sacramentary* (New York: Catholic Book Publishing Company, 1974) 170.

7. Hildegard, in Uhlein, *Meditations* 25.

8. Ibid. 30.

9. Pierre Teilhard de Chardin, "The Mass on the World," in *Hymn of the Universe* (New York: Harper and Row, 1965) 21.

10. From the Green Party Economic Program as cited in Fritjof Capra and Charlene Spretnak, *Green Politics in West Germany: The Global Promise* (New York: E. P. Dutton, Inc., 1984) 93.

11. This myth, from the Hilli Miri tribe is reprinted from *Myths of the Northeast Frontier* of India collected by Verrier Elwin (Arunachal Pradesh, India: Northeast Frontier Agency, 1958) 15.

12. From Penelope Farmer, *Beginnings: Creation Myths of the World* (New York: Atheneum, 1979) 12.

13. This North American Chuhwuht myth is reproduced from Natalie (Curtis) Burlin, *The Indians' Book* (New York: Harper and Brothers, 1907, 1923) 315.

14. From *Kalevala, The Land of Heroes*, vol. 1, trans., W. F. Kirby (London: Dent [Everyman's Library], 1907, 1966) l.

15. Romans 6:3-5. The translation is that of the *New American Bible* (New York: Benziger, 1970).

16. Hildegard, in Uhlein, *Meditations* 63.

17. God speaking in Hiledgard's *Meditations* 31.

18. Loren Eisley, *The Immense Journey* (New York: Vintage Books; Random House, 1957) 15.

19. Quoted on the back cover of *Creation* 1:5 (November-December 1985).

20. An excellent collection of papers by Thomas Berry, called *The Riverdale Papers*, stresses the importance of bioregions as well as topics like planetary management, classical Western spirituality and the American experience, and the spirituality of the earth. These papers are available from the Riverdale Center for Religious Research, 5801 Palisade Ave., Riverdale, New York 10471.

21. In addition to *Green Politics* see Charlene Spretnak, *The Spiritual Dimension of Green Politics* (Santa Fe: Bear and Company, 1986). This is the text of her E. F. Schumacher Lecture.

22. Brian Swimme, "Round Roots, Rounded Roots," *Creation* 1:5 (November-December 1985) 16.

Chapter 4

1. Matthew Fox, *Original Blessing* (Santa Fe: Bear and Company, 1983) 210.

2. Rainer Maria Rilke, *Selected Poems of Rainer Maria Rilke*, trans., Robert Bly (New York: Harper and Row, 1981) 21. Robert Bly calls Rilke the most important poet of the last five hundred years. This selection is from a "Book for the Hours of Prayer."

3. Ecclesiastes 3:1–8 (*New American Bible* translation).

4. Rilke, *Selected Poems* 15.

5. John Ruskin, *Ethics of the Dust*, vol. 18 of *The Works of John Ruskin*, ed., E. T. Cook and Alexander Wedderburn (London: George Allen; New York: Longmans, Green and Co., 1905) 247.

6. See Helen Kenik, "In the Beginning . . . Work," *Creation* 2:2 (May-June 1986) 21–23.

7. For an in-depth discussion of the three stages of our brain development, exercises for using both sides of our creative left/right brain, and helps in "Awakening Your Evolutionary Memory," see Jean Houston, *The Possible Human* (Los Angeles: J. P. Tarcher, Inc., 1982).

8. E. B. White, originally in the *International Herald Tribune*, 13 July 1968, 16. Quoted here from Matthew Fox, *On Becoming a Musical Mystical Bear: Spirituality American Style* (New York: Paulist Press, 1972, 1976) 97.

9. The question of what is more essentially human is often raised in relation to ordination in the Roman Catholic Church. In this context the concern is the maleness of Jesus Christ. Is his maleness essential to his being Messiah? Is the Word made *man* (only) or Word made *flesh* (human)?

10. Phyllis Trible in *God and the Rhetoric of Sexuality* (Philadelphia: Fortress Press, 1978) describes human sexuality as being created with the appearance of Eve; before that there was only the "earth creature." See her chapter "A Love Story Gone Awry." See also Helen Kenik's "Toward a Biblical Basis for Creation Theology" in Fox, ed., *Western Spirituality*.

11. For various treatments of the male/female question, see Mary Daly, *Beyond God the Father* (Boston: Beacon Press, 1973); or Carolyn Heilbrun, *Toward a Recognition of Androgyny* (New York: Knopf, 1973); or Carol Ochs, *Behind the Sex of God* (Boston: Beacon Press, 1977).

Chapter 5

1. From Joseph G. Donders, *Creation and Human Dynamism: A Spirituality for Life* (Mystic, Conn.: Twenty-Third Publications, 1985) 45.

2. Unless otherwise indicated, the translations of the Bible used in this section are taken from the *Inclusive Language Lectionary*, published in three volumes (Year A, 1983; Year B, 1984; Year C, 1985) by the National Council of Churches of Christ in the U.S.A.

3. Swimme, *The Universe* 58.

4. See Fox, *Original Blessing*, Path II.

5. For an excellent telling of this story in relation to the arrival of the Europeans on this continent, see Frederick Turner's *Beyond Georgraphy: The Western Spirit against the Wilderness* (New York: Viking Press, 1980).

6. See Frances Moore Lappé, *Diet for a Small Planet* (New York: Ballantine, 1971, 1975, 1982).

7. Matthew Fox, *A Spirituality Named Compassion and the Healing of the Global Village, Humpty Dumpty and Us* (Minneapolis: Winston Press, 1979) 56.

8. *New American Bible* translation.

9. Thomas Berry, "The Human Venture," *The Riverdale Papers* 2.

10. The Appendix in the *Inclusive Language Lectionary* has the following note: "In this lectionary 'kyrios' generally has been translated 'Sovereign,' a word that also means one supreme in power and authority. It intends no theological difference from 'Lord,' but is free of purely male identification. Women as well as men are sovereigns." (Year A volume)

Part Three

Chapter 6

1. R. Murray Schafer, *Creative Music Education* (New York: Schirmer Books, A Division of MacMillan Publishing Co., 1976) 227.

2. Joanne Romano, who is a cantor at a church in Pittsburgh, once described how the baby in her womb moved differently when she was singing than when he was exposed to external music from the radio or from a record. Beginning in the fourth month, the child expressed through his movements definite preferences for some songs and definite dislike of others.

3. See *Children of a Lesser God,* a play in two acts by Mark Medoff (New Jersey: James T. White and Co., © 1980).

4. Lois Choksy, *The Kodály Method: Comprehensive Music Education from Infant to Adult* (New Jersey: Prentice-Hall, Inc., 1974) 15.

5. In the musical *Sunday in the Park with George* (music and lyrics by Stephen Sondheim, book by James Lapine, New York: Dodd and Mead and Co., 1986, p.196) Dot comments on her choice to leave George (Seurat) and marry Louis:

I chose, and my world was shaken—
So what?
The choice might have been mistaken,
The choosing was not
You have to move on.

6. Some styles of music, like jazz, are essentially improvisatory. This music-making requires incredible, imaginative skills as well as a discipline in using innate talent. These forms are certainly not meant to be excluded from this discussion.

7. Throughout this section the word "movement" is used in the sense of a "movement" in a symphony, one piece of a whole fabric. This word gives us a more organic image than saying "the first step" or "the first level."

8. Irving Stone, *The Agony and the Ecstasy* (New York: Doubleday, 1961) 471.

9. Fox, *Original Blessing* 193.

10. "Furthermore, the New Testament word most often used by Jesus for 'faith' and which Augustine understood as 'intellectual assent'in fact means 'trust' (pisteuein) in the original Greek. Jesus time and again assures people that 'your trust has healed you.'" Fox, *Original Blessing* 83.

Chapter 7

1. Mary Daly, *Beyond God the Father* (Boston: Beacon Press, 1973) 43.
2. T. S. Eliot, "Burnt Norton," *Four Quartets* 15–16.
3. Fox, *Original Blessing* 105.

Chapter 8

1. Chardin, "Pensées" in *Hymn of the Universe* 121.
2. Donders, *Creation and Human Dynamism* 44.
3. 2 Corinthians 5:17–18.
4. Matthew Fox, in a talk given at the National Pastoral Musicians Convention in Detroit, 1981. Printed in *Pastoral Music* 5:5 (June-July 1981) 17.
   5. Donders, *Creation and Human Development* 44.
   6. Remember the Emperor's new clothes?
7. Matthew Fox discusses various reasons why people are afraid to create in chapter four, "Creativity and Compassion," of his book *Compassion*.
   8. Meister Eckhart, in Fox, *Meditations* 82.
9. See Matthew Fox, *Original Blessing*, Theme 16, "Art as Meditation" for the importance of creativity for one's life.
   10. See Philippians 2:6–11.
   11. 1 Corinthians 12:14–21, 26 (*Inclusive Language Lectionary*, Year C, 56).
   12. Mechtild, in Woodruff, *Meditations* 50.

Chapter 9

1. William Dean, *Coming to: A Theology of Beauty* (Philadelphia: Westminster Press, 1972) 188.
2. "To work magic, we begin by making new metaphors. Without negating the light, we reclaim the dark: the fertile earth where the hidden seed lies unfolding, the unseen power that rises within us ... The magic that works is itself a language, a language of action, images, of things rather than abstracts.... Magic speaks to the deep parts of ourselves that we formed before we knew abstractions ... The magic that works is the conscious movement of energy causing changes in accordance with will. Just as tangible things reveal the unseen energies that shape them, the shape and patterns that energy takes in its movement becomes manifest as things." Starhawk, *Dreaming the Dark* 26, 28.
3. The contemporary hospice movement is committed to a more wholesome atmosphere for both the dying persons and those who care for them.
4. I do not wish to say that ritual is *only* music, but that music is ritual just as word, gesture, structure, dance, color, and the like are ritual. What I want to say is that there is a misunderstanding conveyed by talking about

music *and* ritual, or music *in* ritual, or music *for* ritual. Music is not added on for flavor or entertainment but is so integral to ritual that the two cannot be separated. This should make a big difference in our planning.

5. I am grateful to Thomas Stehle for his work in "re-creating" this text.

6. Christopher Fry, *A Sleep of Prisoners* (New York: Oxford University Press, 1951) 47-48.

7. From "Creating Rituals" class, 1985.

Part Four

Chapter 10

1. Casals, *Joys and Sorrows* 60.

2. Rollo May's *The Courage to Create* (New York: W. W. Norton & Co., 1975) is an interesting and very helpful work about the creative process. Carl Jung wrote that "the creative mind plays with the objects it loves" in *Psychological Reflections* (New York: Princeton University Press, 1953) 200.

3. Fox, *Original Blessing* 192.

4. "Often the hands know how to solve a riddle with which the intellect has wrestled in vain." Carl Jung, *Psychological Reflections* 200.

5. Starhawk, *Dreaming the Dark* 35.

Chapter 11

1. Fox, *Original Blessing* 247.

2. Habakkuk 2:2-3 (*New American Bible* translation).

3. For more about the relationship between asceticism and discipline see Fox, *Original Blessing*, Theme 17, "Faith as Trust of Images: Discipline— Yes! Asceticism—No!"

Chapter 12

1. Meister Eckhart, in Fox, *Meditations* 99.

2. Quoted in *Selected Poems of Rainer Maria Rilke*, ed., Robert Bly. Bly attributes his knowledge of this proverb to Walter Spink.

3. See *The Universe Is a Green Dragon*, especially 53-67.